The Contingent Professor

The Contingent Professor

Advice for Adjuncts

Robert Sanford and Daniel Martínez

BEP

BUSINESS EXPERT PRESS

Leader in applied, concise business books

The Contingent Professor: Advice for Adjuncts

First published in 2025 by
Business Expert Press, LLC
222 East 46th Street, New York, NY 10017
www.businessexpertpress.com

ISBN-13: 978-1-63742-802-3 (paperback)
ISBN-13: 978-1-63742-803-0 (e-book)

Business Expert Press Business Career Development Collection

First edition: 2025

10 9 8 7 6 5 4 3 2 1

EU SAFETY REPRESENTATIVE
Mare Nostrum Group B.V.
Mauritskade 21D
1091 GC Amsterdam
The Netherlands
gpsr@mare-nostrum.co.uk

The book is dedicated to our spouses and to the loved ones supporting (often in more ways than one) other folk seeking to survive and even thrive in the contingent world of academia.

Description

Unlock the College Classroom and Make a Lasting Impact

Are you a working professional intrigued by the idea of teaching college students but uncertain about stepping into the role of an adjunct professor? *The Contingent Professor: Advice for Adjuncts* offers a no-nonsense, insider's guide to transforming your knowledge and experience into effective, impactful teaching.

Drawing from insights shared in *The Contingent Professor* podcast, Daniel Martínez and Robert Sanford bring you straight talk, and actionable advice collected from years in the trenches of higher education. This book covers everything an aspiring adjunct needs to know—from engaging students and designing insightful lessons to navigating the academic world as a part-time instructor.

Whether you're a seasoned professional, new to teaching, or already a full-time faculty member looking to deepen your impact, *The Contingent Professor* offers practical strategies to help you overcome challenges, inspire students, and thrive in the classroom. This book empowers you to leave a lasting impact on the next generation of professionals while adding new dimensions to your own career, making every teaching moment meaningful and rewarding.

Contents

Preface

The Contingent Professor: Advice for Adjuncts is for anyone interested in part-time teaching (or eventual full-time teaching) in higher education. It is based on *The Contingent Professor* podcast by Daniel Martínez and Robert Sanford (2016–2022). Mixing practical advice and summaries of literature, it is inspired by *What the Best College Teachers do* (Bain, 2004), *The Effective, Efficient Professor: Teaching, Scholarship, and Service* (Wankat, 2002) and Julie Schumacher's hilarious books that show she really knows the academy, especially *The Shakespeare Requirement* (2018) and *Dear Committee Members* (2014). It is also driven by our experience that every aspiring or current faculty member better look at themselves as if they are contingent if they want to survive. And they better take a good look at what they are getting into. But it can be very rewarding, especially if the instructor has a good idea of what tools are available to promote active learning.

The book is for current and aspiring adjunct faculty but aspires to be equally useful for every teacher or administrator in higher education. It will help administrators and "regular" faculty understand the contingent faculty member and it will help that member prepare for and cope with academia. It will serve working professionals who are considering the idea of teaching a course or two. It might even be useful for graduate students contemplating future careers that could include teaching.

The field of higher education has become even more dynamic since the advent of the COVID pandemic. Consequently, it is particularly useful for professionals contemplating any role in academia to understand current trends and best practices. Each chapter briefly summarizes key aspects and tools in academia. Topics include how to be competitive as a part-timer, the syllabus, common student learner types, classroom techniques, group learning, academic department life, effectiveness and efficiency in teaching and learning, adjunct faculty expectations, experiential learning, use of artificial intelligence (AI), and changing themes in academia.

Acknowledgments

Thanks to Carrie Bell-Howerth, Kristen Cates, Michele Cheung, James C. Golden, Hailey Janelle, Jenna Ledford, James Masi, Lee Ann McLaughlin, Chris Pickles, Michelle Radley, Robin Sanford, Joe Staples, Adam Tuchinsky, Travis Wagner, and Corey Yates for assisting with research, review, and altogether improving this manuscript.

CHAPTER 1

Your Value as a Contingent Professor

So What Is a Contingent Professor Anyway?

From community colleges to elite Ivy League universities, contingent faculty members represent the bulk of the workforce in higher education today. They span a wide variety of positions, including adjuncts, postdocs, graduate assistants, visiting professors, practicum faculty, internship coordinators, clinical faculty, nontenure track research faculty, lecturers, and instructors. The roles, ranks, and titles often vary by institution, reflecting the diversity of needs and organizational priorities within academia.

The term *adjunct*, which you'll see a lot throughout this book, is defined by Cambridge Dictionary as "something added or connected to something larger or more important." It's also a term used to mean "a temporary teacher at a college or university." Adjunct has come to carry a slightly negative connotation in the academy (see the first dictionary definition) and does not encompass all of the roles filled by those in similar positions. So, academics have landed on using the term *contingent faculty* to describe the whole lot. Regardless, adjuncts or contingents typically bring with them specialized expertise that complements the expertise held by the members of an academic department and are brought on by temporary contract. Adjunct lecturers are typically contracted on a semester-by-semester basis without benefits, while other contingents are contracted on an annual or academic year basis. They are hired to address specific departmental needs or to manage excess workload that regular faculty could handle but are otherwise too "engaged" to do so. Increasingly, adjuncts are being brought in to cover a chronic shortage of full-time faculty resulting from shrinking academic revenues and budgets (Nietzel and Ambrose 2024).

Despite their significant contributions to the academy, the role of contingent faculty is often marked by unpredictability. According to the American Association of University Professors, contingent positions are generally "insecure, unsupported positions with little job security and few protections for academic freedom" (AAUP 2023, 1). This instability contrasts with the increasing reliance on such faculty: while only 47 percent of faculty were contingent in 1987, this number had risen to 68 percent by the fall of 2021 (Colby 2023). Given these lopsided figures, we question the definition of "regular" faculty when the majority are, in fact, contingent. These evolving trends highlight the significant shift in academic staffing practices. Beyond that, the demographics of contingent faculty reveal significant inequities. Adjuncts are more likely to be women and underrepresented minorities (Flaherty 2016; Boss, Porter, Davis, and Moore 2021), which underscores broader issues of representation and fairness within higher education.

All of this is to say: if you are contingent, you are in good company. But you are also part of a larger discussion about the evolution and challenges of academic labor in modern universities. There are plenty of books that discuss in detail the inequities associated with being an adjunct. This book is not one of them. The purpose of this book is to educate professionals on how to enter higher education as an instructor free from expectations that it will turn into a full-time gig. The odds of that happening are just way too low, and people who stick around trying to "beat the system" are usually miserable after just a few years.

Why You Are Needed in Higher Education

Your role as an adjunct/contingent is much more important to your future department than just filling in academic gaps. Working professionals bring with them an expertise that enriches the student learning experience beyond what the in-house academics can typically provide. Your contributions are especially valuable in linking theory to the "real world." It is very powerful for students to have a teacher who can explain the "why" and the "how" as well as the "what," helping students understand the relevance and importance of their academic studies. Perhaps most important to current students is that working professionals tend to have active networks and can connect them with employers —you might even hire one to work for you.

One thing is certain: adjunct positions generally do not pay well, but despite that, there are good reasons to be an adjunct. Here are six nonmonetary reasons:

1. Faculty get pleasure and enjoyment out of seeing students engaged in something they care about. You get to be a part of that.
2. Holding a teaching position lends a certain prestige to a resume —and carries value beyond monetary pay.
3. You are contributing to the community and your discipline in particular, and to the general good of the country through promoting education.
4. Potential collaborations and connections can enrich your personal and professional life.
5. It informs your career; you get insights into your life choices. Being an adjunct helps in seeing if you want to become a full-time academic. Plus, you'll need teaching experience to be seriously considered.
6. You get a free university library card. That is to say, gaining access to university resources for a writing project or personal research you are developing can be extremely valuable.
7. You are benefiting the academic institution. Yes, this might not be high on your priority list, but it does reflect the fact that this is a two-way street, and most institutions realize this; they need you.

Time and Title

Full-time professorships at universities are often based on research and/or creative work and publishing rather than on teaching, even if the job is, ironically, a teaching position. This seems to be the case even if the advertised position is based on one-third teaching, one-third research, and one-third service. This bias often disqualifies professionals who, even if they are amazing teachers, may lack the "proof" of research/creative work and publication. At a two-year college, which generally accounts for most jobs anyway, the emphasis will be on teaching, as usually there are not any research expectations. This should make it a little easier to break into a full-time position should you be tempted. Teaching is the baseline expectation. Research is the anticipated value-added. Note, however, that some full-time faculty jobs do not involve research and are explicitly identified as such in their titles, like "Professor of Practice," or "Teaching Professor," or "Lecturer."

A significant number of adjuncts do not want to teach full time. They prefer the flexibility of part-time work and avoiding the "politics" of academia. They also find that it contributes to their other work, which remains their primary profession and emphasis. Wallis (2013) makes a case for the move from adjunct professor to adjunct entrepreneur rather than moving to full-time academia. This makes sense since there are relatively few pathways to go from part time to full time. But some faculty already employed full time at one institution will be contingent at another, as much for a safety net as for anything else (Carlson 2021).

The Pressure to Say "Yes"

Contingent professors may feel the pressure to say yes to additional classes offered to them (even if it's a huge time commitment) because they fear losing their next contract offer if they don't. Of course, they might not think of this as pressure, since in the short term, it provides income and opportunity. However, there is a risk from "stretching" themselves to fit the desires of the university. Contingents are more likely than others to be asked to teach courses outside of their "home" department or field, large section classes, unpopular time slots, and online. This can make them seem more attractive, versatile, and amenable to the hiring institution, but there are energy and time costs to doing this.

As we already mentioned, being contingent does have its benefits. The upside of contingent teaching is the freedom that your full-time colleagues will envy (unambitious, tenured full professors notwithstanding). Typically, this means no committee requirements, no advising requirements, no department meetings, no college service, and, other than classes, you can make your own schedule. People interested in pursuing more in-depth college connections, possibly chasing the allure of a full-time position, might aim for some service responsibilities. If you are one of those people we caution you about accepting service work, those are a true time suck and should only be considered if you enjoy volunteering for volunteering's sake.

Even if not anticipating further involvement, it still might be useful to attempt attending some department meetings and functions that occur while you are on campus, especially during times of change and upheaval. Attending these scheduled meetings can keep you informed of departmental dynamics and impactful institutional changes, keeping you apprised of new policies or shifts in direction that could affect your courses or your role in the department. Within a well-functioning department, your opinion and insight at these meetings will likely be requested and recognized, helping to influence upcoming decisions.

Are You Qualified to Work in Higher Ed?

Most adjuncts have a graduate degree of some sort. Actually, one-third of adjuncts hold a doctorate, usually a PhD (Yakobski 2019). So, having a PhD is pretty standard and not particularly special. We don't mean to hurt anyone's feelings, but let's get that out of the way first. The PhD is the entry-level calling card for full-time, tenure-track higher education faculty at four-year institutions, of which there are nearly 4,000 in the United States. Some people think that a PhD is a guaranteed academic job, but it is not—just consider the high numbers of people with PhDs saturating the market. There are about 10 or more PhDs for every one tenure-track position. Even in engineering, it is just one tenure-track job for 12.8 percent of new PhD graduates (Larson, Ghaffarzadegan, and Xue 2014). Or look at the doctoral-level tenured faculty who have lost their positions (Carlson 2021). If you don't think that is true, post on LinkedIn with a job advertisement and you will see what we mean.

If you have a doctorate, we hope you obtained it for its own sake. Academic doctorates usually are not a great return on investment for nontenure-track faculty, especially for those in the engineering fields where industry is the most likely landing spot for good work and a better salary. Whether or not you have a doctorate, remember, the academy wants people who can deliver the goods. For some fields and institutions, this may mean a doctoral minimum requirement for adjunct professor positions and a master's or equivalent for adjunct lecturers and instructors. It varies by how competitive the market is, as well as by what is considered essential. Ultimately, what counts is what is in the job description advertised. Only candidates who meet the minimum will be passed from Human Resources (HR) to the hiring department or committee.

Dirty Secret: Most New Professors Are "Worse Than Average" at Teaching

In Felder and Brent's *Teaching and Learning STEM: A Practical Guide* (2016), the opening chapter starts, "welcome to the university, there's your office, good luck." Sounds familiar? As an adjunct entering the arena, it may be helpful for you to realize that the "regular" professors are not trained in the many facets of their jobs prior to arriving at their first university post. Graduate students are typically taking upper-level coursework in their specific field and trained how to do scholarship by their mentors in a very narrow subfield. There usually isn't any time in graduate school to learn how to prepare a syllabus for teaching, to learn the finer aspects of evolving pedagogy, or how to find resources to help a student struggling in their class. Most graduate students never study teaching as a formal subject; it's almost always through mimicry or on-the-job experience (Wankat 2002).

Regardless of the educational background of a prospective contingent faculty member, if she has been working in industry for 10 years or more, she is likely to be in the same proverbial "boat" as a freshly minted assistant professor. In fact, this breadth of experience provides a tremendous advantage over the new assistant professor. The ability to draw from practical work experience is exactly why you are sought after by the more conscientious department chairs.

What Does Your Degree Mean to the Institution?

Most adjuncts have either an academic or professional master's degree or higher. After all, if the academy doesn't respect and expect formal education, then who else will? Most four-year and graduate institutions require a master's degree of some kind. Many two-year institutions also require a master's degree but may allow only a bachelor's degree, along with relevant experience. Competition for adjunct positions is increasing in some fields. You will see doctorates as quite common at many two-year schools.

Someone considering teaching in the humanities or fine arts should have a bachelor's or master's, particularly a BFA or MFA—a studio arts professor is a good example of such. However, with no licensing requirement for artists and authors, their own track records will be sufficient to establish their authority as adjunct faculty. No one is going to tell Stephen King[*] that he needs a PhD to teach an adjunct course on writing at the University of Maine.

Job Tip: Read up on Your Future Co-Workers

If you hold degrees from institutions similar to those of the faculty in the department you are interested in joining, it can help you make connections with them. It can also make it easier for them to see what you "bring to the table." But if your degrees and institutions are markedly different, that can be a strength too because you will

---

[*] Stephen King, one of the world's best-selling authors, has a BA in English from the University of Maine, which has an endowed professorship, the Stephen E. King Chair in Literature, in his honor.

be adding to the diversity. Your approach in this case is that diversity of background means more varied capabilities and abilities, which are adaptive in dealing with today's changing environment in higher education. Either way, check the faculty pages on university websites for where and when people trained. It provides a useful insight into the department you would like to work for.

This is a good time to clear up something we frequently come across: reference to "ABD." An ABD means "all but dissertation" and is sometimes confused with being an actual degree. It does mean that someone was on the road toward getting an academic doctorate. But it doesn't necessarily mean that they are still making progress. Far more people start a doctorate than ever finish it. You may want to avoid using or referring to ABD in your resume and correspondence. It is far better to refer to having had additional courses or to state that you are in a doctoral program or still working on a doctorate, especially if you are applying for a temporary teaching gig. But if the job description or qualifications you are interested in use the term *ABD* and you happen to be one, then yes, go ahead and use that.

Finally, the academy respects professional licenses and certificates. If you do not have a master's degree but are a licensed professional engineer (PE) or are a registered nurse (RN), for example, you already know that has meaning outside of the academic world, but you can feel equally assured of your qualifications in academia. This is increasingly true as the academy becomes ever more pragmatic and ever more reliant on adjuncts. Students are more likely than ever before to want to know why they are learning what they are learning. Your professional licenses, training, and certificates can help them know about the practical application of their learning. Many accrediting bodies also require a certain number of faculty to hold professional certifications. Use that to your advantage.

Advantages for Institutions

Before the overreliance on contingent faculty became widely reported as a problem in higher education, universities and colleges had used (and continue to use) temporary hires to fill voids and to allow departments to experiment with new offerings. Indeed, there are monetary and strategic advantages to utilizing contingent faculty, more so for teaching undergraduate and graduate students but also for rounding out research programs and keeping in good standing with accreditation requirements.

Most of the monetary advantages are either tied to money that institutions can save by paying a part-time instructor much less than a full-time professor for the same teaching service or tied to attracting new student enrollments through unique course offerings and/or "rock star" professionals. Especially in large metropolises such as Los Angeles, Chicago, or New York, you have a massive population to draw from and have a massive pool of prominent CEOs, lawyers, MBAs, and tech entrepreneurs who could be enticed to teach a class of 500 would-be professionals. The gravity of their standing will attract new students to take that class. Ultimately, departments are judged by how many credit hours they generate and how much that adds to a university's or a college's bottom line.

We'll assume that most professionals reading this book are not of the Fortune 500 kind that we were speaking of in the previous paragraph, and that's OK. The value that the rest of us bring is through our experiences as professionals in the local community or through long, successful careers. Adjuncts who are lawyers, small business owners, public servants, or inventors still provide rich value to a university. A local landscape architect, for example, would be able to provide a very worthwhile upper-level course to a smaller academic department. Warning: Some tenured faculty members might push back at having you on the books if your course becomes too popular—they might fear losing student enrollment in their obscure upper-level niche course and do not want any more uninvited attention to being compared to you.

The strategic institutional advantages of using contingent faculty are twofold. Regarding teaching, Guthrie, Wyrick, and Navarette (2019) say that adjuncts help universities and colleges maintain a flexible labor pool, which is strategically useful during times of budgetary problems or during times of rapidly changing student demand. Regarding other academic roles such as those of research faculty or new program directorships, it allows for rapid response to national funding calls both in research and in workforce training.

Demanding Students

Student demand is an especially interesting consideration in higher education today. It can be measured in several ways. There may be a demand for new courses and degrees in hot button topics such as artificial intelligence (AI), forever chemicals, or climate change, which lends itself to recruiting outside experts to teach a class on the subjects. There may also be a demand for small class sizes, in which case more sections of the same class are capped at no more than, say, 15 students. This affords additional opportunities for adjunct instruction. Finally, there may be a local industry that operates in a critical area of regional or national importance, and demand for trained professionals will spur state and federal funding to implement new programs to handle critical shortages or to address an expected future need. Institutions that react and respond to these varying demands will invariably reach out to a contingent workforce to help staff courses for instruction.

Enhancing Institutional Prestige and Competitiveness

Since its inception in 1983, U.S. News and World Report's college rankings list has codified the way to improve institutional prestige and competitiveness at a national level. This list has the power to make or break a school's reputation, especially for those trying to climb into the elite top 20 tier. The ranking system has long been tied to data provided by ranked institutions and invites gaming (see Kutner 2014). Of the various ranking scores, the most important at the undergraduate level seem to be:

- Graduation and retention rates
- Acceptance rate (i.e., selectivity)
- SAT scores (the SAT was removed as a criterion in college admissions but is being reinstated in admissions decisions);
- Number of full-time faculty
- Class size
- Reputation via peer reviews

These metrics are extremely important to private colleges and universities across the country, and you can guarantee a rebuttal by top college administrators to any drop in rankings year to year. State schools are favored a bit more in the most current ranking analysis, but top-tier research universities are also mindful of what they must do to receive a favorable score among their peer institutions.

It will be interesting to see how much this, or any other college ranking system, will consider metrics that are more easily controllable by academic institutions, such as class size and number of full-time faculty, in light of the changing reality of hiring part-time adjuncts and other contingent faculty across the board. Beyond national prestige, however, there is a legitimate need for local colleges and universities to be competitive in the local landscape, both to keep local high school talent that inevitably will want to attend a top 20 school and also to attract students from outside the state or region.

Short of receiving a multimillion-dollar donation from an anonymous donor (think George Eastman and MIT), what a local, regional university can do is attract part-time talent that are well known by that population. Some members of the local community may have achieved significant success in their fields, and bringing them into the academy on even a part-time basis brings good publicity and recognized expertise to a university. This is fairly clear in something like having an internationally recognized author teach a graduate seminar course in the English department. But it is also an opportunity for engineering, technology, business, the legal community, and any number of other fields and professions.

Preserving Organizational Flexibility

Academic units benefit from the use of adjuncts by achieving organizational flexibility because the movement in and out of adjuncts is much more fluid and economical than creating or bringing in permanent (usually tenure track) positions or eliminating them—both sources of stress economically and organizationally. It allows departments and institutions to be opportunistic when a chance relationship forms, either by a relocation of a professional to the region, a targeted donation, or a rapid response to an area of national importance. Even in an atmosphere of tight budgets, this could be a relatively low-cost investment that could bear significant fruit either through new enrollments, positive press, or perhaps even establishing a nationally recognized program.

Serving the Community

Academic institutions have a reputation as "ivory towers" somehow separate from the community around them. Often referred to as some sort of "town–gown" dichotomy, this separation preserved a sense of independence hard to justify in these times. Institutions are generally growing their community-serving opportunities such as civic engagement courses, internships, and programs that serve their surrounding communities. Similarly, providing an employment magnet for adjuncts is a form of service because, in such cases, the adjuncts are drawn from a local pool; no one is going to pull up stakes and move for a one-semester, one-course teaching opportunity.

Over the years, we've heard more than once from academic deans that the key to unlocking more funding for our small department was to create a large lecture course that everyone would want to attend. The phrasing was always something a little different, but it essentially was, "if you build a class that attracts 100 new students, then we can talk about providing more funding to your department." Clearly, these administrators have been reading too many education trade journals that highlight such a class being developed at NYU or Stanford and think that it could be applied to any institution anywhere regardless of budget concerns. In fact, there are a great deal of smaller, local, and low-cost solutions that can help bolster an institution's prestige and enrollments, given the right leadership and the right, targeted investment.

Trends and Challenges

Many students in the United States now go to college because they need it to get a good job. Not that long ago, a high school degree was the benchmark or bar of achievement for students. Then it was the college associate or baccalaureate degree. But so many people get college degrees now that bar too has risen, and higher degrees are needed to get the same position as before. Interestingly, there has been a backlash, with some people questioning the value of a college degree at all. This is compounded by the increasing cost of higher education and the increased availability of lower-cost "coding camps" or jobs that pay wages like what a student might earn upon graduation. The number and size of student loans is staggering compared to what a degree can provide for career wage earnings.

Higher education is working to overcome past trends that reflect passive or active discrimination. STEM (Science, Technology, Engineering, and Mathematics) programs must work harder to attract more females and underrepresented minorities. The fine arts programs must include information for students to be able to communicate as artists and act as their own business agents. Service programs (teaching, clergy, social work, and related) numbers have decreased. "Time to completion of degree" (a common variable used in assessment) has increased on average. Preference for two-year schools over four-year schools has increased. Students are more interested in getting degrees for occupational credentials than for academic credentials.

Reasons for the Rise in Cost

Rising higher education costs are typically attributed to the need to invest in modern facilities and more personnel (faculty and staff) who

> demand competitive wages and health benefits. New dining halls, new gym facilities, smaller class sizes, and more student and career services are hallmarks of a "quality" institution, where competition is fierce for student tuition payments to cover these costs. Gone are the days of society valuing education for itself—just look at the decline in state-funded allocations and increase in tuition revenue at public colleges and universities.

This is a major driving force for the increased reliance on a contingent workforce in higher ed. Roughly 60 percent of a university's operational costs go to faculty and staff salaries and benefits (TopUniversities 2024). This number would grow a little each year as it tracks inflation and increased health care costs if it weren't for colleges increasing revenue via increased tuition fees or by other fundraising. So, we can expect fewer tenure-track positions, meaning graduate students will have to pursue nontraditional careers outside of academia. With that, we can expect a decline in the percentage of tenured professors.

We can also expect increased demand for accountability in academia. Departments will have to do more to justify course offerings and enrollments. Revenue pressures will increase. Services might go down. Outside grant funding will be ever more important but ever harder to get. Demand for demonstrable skills will grow faster than the demand for abstract knowledge as students are more interested in getting degrees for occupational credentials than for academic credentials.

Discriminatory Skills

Students have an increased need for discriminatory skills at the introductory level. For prior generations, the task in writing an undergraduate paper boiled down to finding references in the library. Then later, they learned how to discriminate among references to find what was true, but at least the journals and books had gone through some sort of vetting by librarians to get into the collection. Now the student simply types a few search words, and tens of thousands of sources appear instantly. But there is little vetting of such materials.

Information literacy has become increasingly important. Gooblar (2019, 200) cites a study in which students were readily "fooled by the trappings of pseudo-authority" on websites. "Lateral reading" means checking other research to help assess the credibility of a source. Further, we are experiencing increased distrust of science and academia (Boyle 2022). Generative AI will only magnify this problem. Yet the world has to deal with increasingly complex information and challenges. Everyone needs to become a fact checker as part of participating in capacious issues like climate change. Perhaps the most important thing a professor can do for students is to encourage their information literacy through the development and employment of critical thinking skills.

Community Connections

We might see an increase in the community connections of colleges—particularly public institutions for whom it is clearly a dominant part of their "social contract," with greater internships, partnerships, part-time instructors, and other involvement in the community. The community is interested in basic skills and the ability to learn because it enriches the community and is good for the local economy. Area businesses have been some of the biggest champions of basic skills in writing and mathematics because they recognize these as building blocks for skills and abilities ("soft skills" and technical skills). Theoretical knowledge is an important part of applied knowledge, and higher education knows how to impart both. The liberal and fine arts are also pathways to critical thinking recognized as valuable for a nation of employable, life-long learners. Contingent faculty are well-positioned to fuel the connections to critical thinking and to community.

Separation From Regular Faculty

Although adjuncts and other contingents are part of an academic department, if they have been contracted to teach a class, like an introductory lecture course, seminar, or lab, it is very unlikely that they will interact much with regular faculty. This is especially true if they are working in a large service department such as Mathematics, Biology, or English. There are just too many students, too many course sections, too many administrative tasks, and too little time for regular faculty to go out of their way to befriend a part-timer who may not be around after the semester. Even in smaller departments, contingents will likely only interact with the academic chair, the administrative assistant (AA), and perhaps one other faculty member (e.g., the one that manages the lab curriculum for the department). It's not that regular faculty are unfriendly (though some definitely are); it's just that they are busy trying to meet all of their teaching, research, and service commitments; and also trying to get home to watch their kid's little league game.

Figuring Things Out on Your Own

It is very likely that you, as an instructor, will be expected to figure out how to do things on your own. This fact is well known and difficult to remedy given the low priority faculty in general take up at a college. It is almost always about the students and what they need and want. With part-timers potentially working after regular business hours, figuring things out is even more pronounced. It's ironic, of course, because faculty are the people who interface with the students most, yet often are considered to be cogs in the delivery of promised curriculum.

Despite this reality, contingent faculty still need support, and good departments do their best to provide some, with the department chair or a faculty liaison taking that lead. Academic Impressions (2012), a private company that consults to colleges and universities across the United States and Canada, identifies key areas where contingent faculty need support, including:

1. Thorough and engaging orientation
2. Needs-based training
3. "Just-in-time" support
4. Purposeful steps to foster adjuncts' sense of belonging
5. Relevant and engaging ongoing professional development

6. Meaningful recognition

If the department you work for does not provide these types of support, it is advised to be proactive and ask for them. Academics tend to bury their heads in the sand but will come up to assist if asked directly.

Being Present in the Office

As an adjunct, you may receive pressure to be present on campus more than it may feel reasonable given the one course you are teaching. Where is this coming from? Fitzgerald (2017) notes that many schools are becoming "ghost towns." These empty halls are not just devoid of students; they are also devoid of faculty. Even before COVID, students had begun coming in only for class (and sometimes not even then). This tends to be worse in public universities with multiple campuses and a primarily commuter student body. Also, due to remote teaching and learning, connecting is possible now with technology. Furthermore, everything is more easily done without going into the office. Even faculty find it more productive to do scholarly work from home or in their lab to free themselves from the distraction of students (and of emeritus professors who no longer know how to function in normal society).

Institutions are trying to increase faculty presence, in the hope that this will improve community and build student presence. As an adjunct, you may be vulnerable to such pressure, but it is easily handled by keeping within the confines of what is necessary and appropriate to deliver your course. You can expect to have maybe one hour a week either before or after each class, either in person or virtually, or some other arrangement, and deliver a perfectly fine course.

Student Hours

The time in office you allocate to seeing students was probably called "office hours" when you were in college but is gradually becoming known as "student hours" in an effort to be more student friendly. It's a good idea for you to go ahead and call them student hours on your syllabi and post them on your course site and office door, even if your contract still refers to them as office hours. Consider having them be just before or just after your class meetings so you don't have to make any extra trips to campus. Also, allow some virtual time and "to be arranged" time so you provide flexibility to students with tight schedules. A couple of hours a week should be sufficient for a three-credit course. If you have a shared office space, you may have to relocate to the library or some other more private space to maintain student confidentiality.

Salary

Unlike the professional adjunct who is cobbling together teaching opportunities for their primary salary, the working professional accepts that they are being underpaid and undervalued by the institution but tolerates it because they know it is not their day job and they derive satisfaction from the classroom, that is, teaching an interesting topic to (mostly) interested students. Always keep this in mind and accept that universities look to the contingent workforce primarily to save money on labor and health care and secondarily to support an experimental class that might attract new students. In both scenarios, a one-class flier on a contingent faculty member is much cheaper than a contract offer to a full-time professor or lecturer. And if you are an effective instructor and popular with the students, you are providing immense value to the university, but more importantly to the department you are working for.

Can I Negotiate?

While it is tempting to just say no, contingents do have some power to negotiate. People applying for full-time academic jobs have a little bit more power. For both, this power probably depends on the rigidity of the institution, the market value of new graduates in the subject area you teach, your "standing" in academia or industry, and the proximity to other colleges or universities that may be interested in having you teach that class for a higher sum of money (i.e., a competing offer).

Kelsky (2017) points out that job applicants can still engage in negotiation even if they do not have competing offers. Usually, departments do not want to rescind offers because, academia being among the most bureaucratic of bureaucracies, it took them nearly forever to get the job approved in the first place. But if it is only a part-time position in a high buyer-demand field, departments are likely to just move on to the next candidate. This is not typically good news for English teachers. But then if you are an English teacher, you already know that.

Many academic institutions, particularly public ones, have only very limited flexibility in salary offers. The salary range will have been cleared through HR after a lengthy process. Offering a salary for a part-time lecturer, which is proportionately higher than what many full-time people of higher academic rank make, would cause significant labor issues and unrest among the current employees. The institution is trying to get as much as they can for as little as they can. Academia often lags behind others in salaries and compensation for the professoriate, to put it mildly.

Some deans will offer as high as they can on the salary range for the initial offer and won't have any leeway to negotiate. Other deans will try to get the adjuncts for as low as possible. How do you know which one you are dealing with? Chances are, as a working professional choosing to moonlight in the academy, you probably are not doing it for the money. But you do have to maintain your self-respect. The best you can do is background research. If it is a public institution, the salaries and ranges will be a matter of public record. For private schools, you can probably get similar information at the nearest pub or coffee house.

You should be able to research the hiring institution's practices and check its reputation—you probably would have done this already as part of deciding if you want to apply there in the first place. If it is a full-time position, tenure-track or lecturer, you can be reassured in knowing that the department is making a choice about a long-term colleague and therefore is vested in having you accept the offer they've made. If you are contingent, be assured in knowing that over half the curricula in today's colleges are delivered by contingent faculty, and the academic department is vested in having you deliver the same quality of instruction as their other members. Furthermore, many contingent faculty, once they get through the first semester or two, gain a presumptive right of employment to continue teaching courses in their area of qualification, particularly at public institutions.

Where to Look for Jobs

There are lots of places to check for academic jobs. Many colleges and universities have notification requirements that cause jobs to be listed on local publications as well as on college websites. HigherEdJobs, AdjunctWorld, VirtualVocations, Academic Careers.com, LinkedIn, ZipRecruiter, Indeed.com, a subject-based listserv and professional societies, The Chronicle of Higher Education, individual and system universities and colleges, and many other sources list jobs or provide notifications.

There may be some flexibility in the compensation for particular types of courses and teaching circumstances. You can assume, however, that any front-loading work you do, such as developing lectures for a new course (or a course for which no previous material is available), is done on your own time, so you should consider whether there are options to teach the course more than once or if it is worth it for just the one time. Laboratory and practicum courses often require the same amount of work and contact time as lecture courses but are billed as fewer credits and therefore pay less. It may be possible to negotiate extra compensation for teaching these courses, as the academic departments will be aware of this issue. You might also negotiate some things that you think are essential for delivering the course, such as laboratory supplies that are not already in inventory.

The Types of Courses You Can Expect to Teach

As a professional who presumably earned a degree or two, you may recall the basic types of college courses:

- First-year seminars
- General education courses (or "core" courses)
- Major-specific courses
- Electives
- Laboratory courses
- Studio courses
- Independent study courses
- Orientation courses

Formats can include: lecture, discussion, or remote/online delivery, either live in real time, asynchronous, or as a hybrid course partially in person and partially online.

An adjunct lecturer is usually hired to teach a specific course, possibly multiple sections of that course. Once you are hired, the academic department may have other courses you can teach. Most departments have a course rotation schedule, anywhere from two to five years. This is probably published somewhere online, but most likely printed out and on a table or file folder in the department office. If you do manage to find it online (universities are notorious for making it difficult for the public to find updated content on their websites), access it and see what courses you might like to teach if you want to be proactive about further teaching for that department. Some academic department chairs are just waiting to hear that you are interested in teaching other courses. Others will be proactive in asking you about it. Either way, no harm is done in letting them know of your interests and abilities because getting courses scheduled and taught is often a chair's biggest headache.

Get Ready to Teach Intro Courses

As a contingent professor, you are presumably prepared to teach whatever course they need you for. This will be skewed by a variety of factors. Most professors are far more interested in teaching small class size, upper-level courses that match well with what they conduct research on or perform scholarly work in than they are in teaching a 200-student first-year lecture course on a general introductory topic. Introductory classes that are meant to satisfy a university's core curriculum, such as freshman writing courses, the college algebra requirement, or the general science requirement (Geology 101, anybody?) are often not well regarded by students, because half or more may not be taking it as part of their intended major. It can be difficult to engage those students when they'd rather be learning something directly tied to their degree program, or they think that they are relearning material from high school (even though they likely never internalized it in the first place). Intro classes are the lowest-hanging fruit for adjuncts to grab. You may think that your expertise in nuclear reactor theory would make for an interesting 400-level course, but it's that Intro to Physics lab that will get you the university gig. Once in the system, you may not only find your offered selection of courses increases, but you may also find reward in teaching even the courses that other professors avoid, because you will have mastered the challenge of the course and the students.

If you are teaching courses with multiple sections, find out who the other instructors are and consider meeting with them to coordinate various aspects of the course, including student performance expectations. A good academic department will likely be offering opportunities and guidance for this. Teaching multiple sections of the same course provides a much greater opportunity for efficiency of time. If you are teaching two sections of the same course, your preparation essentially reduces in half, especially if you can keep the same pace in each section. You may have different classroom management concerns; however, since all classes have their own "personality." In all, teaching multiple sections becomes a more practical use of your time and skills, although it would be less of a variety.

Syllabus Expectations

One benefit of teaching an introductory course is that the syllabus has likely already been developed and a textbook already vetted for use with the class or lab. You will find there are expected items, cautions, policies, advice, and such to be included in the syllabus that they are now monstrosities of a dozen or more pages. Essentially, a syllabus represents a contract, a covenant between you (representing "the academy") and the student. We will have more advice on syllabi, but at this stage know that it is quite possibly due before you are even given your contract. The department chair will be your best guide on this, but for now, consider it a place where you want to clearly articulate what you will do, how you will do it, and how you will assess your students. You should be able to get copies of syllabi used for previous versions of the course. If not, look for sample syllabi for other courses the department offers so you can gauge the tone and variation.

Getting a Second Offer

Finally, know that if you have obtained a regularly offered course and opt out of teaching it one time, there is a good chance you will get off the roster (real or mental) and not be offered to teach it again. (This has happened to us before.) The chance of being asked again after once declining depends on how in-demand your services are, what your field is, and other market forces, including how pressured a department chair is in ensuring that a course is "covered."

Conclusion

Okay, you have been hired to teach a course. Congratulations, you are now a member of "the academy," and most of your students will see you as that, manifested in a single dimension—their professor. They are unlikely to care about your actual title; who is a full professor, visiting professor, research professor, associate professor, practicum coordinator, assistant professor, lecturer, or instructor. We need to be careful that administrators do not find this out, as it could be used as an argument to keep professors at a lower rank or to not give tenure. Seriously though, students most likely will be looking to you as the subject expert regardless of your title and as a representative of the college or university. So, you have to jump into things quickly and with authority.

As you are getting acclimated, become fast friends with the department AA. The AA is the hub of getting things done and presumably your most important contact. The other professors will be relieved that you have been hired to cover a course and will have moved on to their own priorities and concerns. The department chair may still be available to help, but they too will be working through and depending on the AA. If the university onboarding procedure has an orientation, they will likely provide you with a list of what things you need to do and what resources are available to help you do them. You will need to think of some of these things right away as they affect institutional access and course planning and delivery. You'll be mostly on your own after this time.

One thing for certain is that academic institutions are changing the way courses are delivered and who is teaching them. There is much greater use of technology, remote teaching and learning, and increased use of contingent faculty. Degree programs are more fluid than ever, with increasing part-time degree opportunities, partnerships, and other creative learning formats. Increasingly, academic institutions are recognizing their need to be part of their surrounding communities and the draw of the communities in supplying academics that can help deliver core programs and supplement the institutional offerings. This makes it an exciting and opportune time to become part of an academic department as a teacher or in another part-time role.

Working as an adjunct is a way to get a taste of academia without the commitment of leaving your job. It lets you make a significant contribution to student education and gives you a role in the more optimistic of all acts: helping someone learn something. Most people who are contingent faculty are not seeking entry into a full-time position, but there are always some who want to go this route either because they discover they really like teaching or because they are not able to find a full-time position. We tend to agree with Wright (2019). He says not to waste your time fooling around as an adjunct or a visiting professor. Instead, develop your skills and reputation outside of academia. Then aim full time at getting into a professor position. He realizes that not everyone will concur with his recommendation and that market factors may mean people sometimes have little other choice. And we didn't take his recommended approach either, so we figure there is a good chance you are like us, noodling around as a way of getting started. And that is one reason why we have written this book.

Keep Coming Back

By the end of my first year of adjuncting, I concluded that academia is like a government bureaucracy staffed with highly educated and highly selfish megalomaniacs. Professors think they are the smartest people in the room. Rather, each professor thinks he or she is the smartest person in the room and everybody else is an idiot. That is, until the classroom computer and overhead projector stop working—then you'll witness a panicked child screaming for help from IT to fix it for them. And yet, I kept coming back when they asked me to teach another course.

CHAPTER 2

Understanding the Organization and Hierarchy of Higher Ed

Higher Education Fuzziness: Some Key Concepts

The vocabulary of higher education is extensive and as we embark on this journey as a contingent faculty member, it is helpful to understand the most salient features of the academic organizational structure and the higher education hierarchy. As a teaser, be prepared to be called "professor" more often than not, "Mr." or "Mrs." on occasion, and sometimes you will be called by your first name, which can be welcomed by faculty in some departments and reviled by faculty in others. Also, higher education is very much a rank and status game.

We Don't Teach, We Profess

Yes, we know faculty teach in college, but K-12 schools also have faculties with members who teach. So, what is the difference between teachers and professors? In higher education, the professors usually do not have a degree in education (except in schools or programs of education). This means they are not fully trained in how students learn. That training is held by K-12 teachers. Indeed, higher education faculty *profess* and K-12 teachers *teach*. It is assumed that by the time students get to college they already know how to learn, so they only need experts in subject areas: professors.

Professors usually have a degree in what they are professing about or in something reasonably related. They typically do not have a degree in education unless that is the field they are teaching about. The assumption is that professors do not normally need a degree in education because students who are in college should have spent their earlier years (K-12) learning *how* to learn and by now are ready to focus on *what* to learn, thus needing experts in content ("professors" who profess a subject) rather than experts in both pedagogy and content (let's call them "teachers"). However, students in college often do not enter knowing how to be successful learners, although the entrance requirements mean theoretically, they have the ability to be just that. Further muddying the waters, professors are also called teachers. Consider this a compliment. Good professors know how students learn and can teach them to improve how they learn.

Finally, the American Federation of Teachers (AFT), the National Education Association (NEA), and the American Association of University Professors all represent college faculty, even though AFT and NEA are primarily conceived of as K-12 teacher unions. So it is fair to consider professors as teachers in the grand scheme of things; however, the title means something else, if not more.

Tenure? They Still Do That?

Outside of academia, people often either do not understand tenure or think it is some sort of magical endowment that prevents faculty from all accountability. Some institutions use contracts of various lengths for full-time faculty, but most still use tenure. If you are a part-time person not intending to pursue a full-time academic career, why do you even care about tenure? Because as a teaching member of the department you are a cog in the system. Much of the curriculum is usually delivered by nontenured faculty and the balance of this is an ongoing discussion. But for many institutions tenure is the academic brass ring, despite tarnishing on that ring. If you are going to be on campus, virtual or actual, you are going to hear about it. You will benefit from knowing the basics.

In short, tenure means a faculty member is vested in the system and the presumption is that they are doing their job. A tenure-track position has the end goal of becoming tenured. Someone who is not yet tenured has to deal with the presumption that they must show they are doing their job because they do not yet enjoy the presumption that they are doing their job. Tenure is really a right to due process.

During the pretenure annual review, the faculty member makes the case that they are doing their job adequately so their peer committee can recommend "overcoming" the presumption that they are not doing the job of a professor, based on some loosely codified standards. Since the presumption shifts *after* tenure, the college cannot fire a professor without evidence of the professor not doing their job (or behaving criminally). Or so the theory goes. But, as recessions have shown us, the college can, under the rules of financial exigency, eliminate the job the professor was in, and even the entire department (Carlson 2021). Poof, in such cases that faculty member is gone (and perhaps even that entire department is), and so is their respective tenure. They weren't fired so much as their position was permanently eliminated. Tenure just means they likely got some sort of severance.

Also, tenured faculty still get reviewed for promotion or periodically to verify they are still doing their jobs, known as post-tenure review. Tenure also carries certain other privileges such as the ability to apply for and receive paid sabbaticals, to stay in the job indefinitely as long as the job still exists, and perhaps most notably, it allows them to complain about administrators and other faculty, without fear of significant recourse.

The arguments for and against tenure are well established. Writing in the *Harvard Business Review,* James Wetherbe (2013) summarizes arguments against tenure:

- Tenure is outdated—it was a response to an 18th-century issue that has gone away.
- Tenure has become a "guaranteed" job—a phenomena not seen in any other job sector.
- Many countries outside of the United States have already gotten rid of tenure.
- U.S. schools are already losing ground (lost spots on lists of superior colleges, losing publications, etc.,) and therefore need to act against tenure.

- Tenure locks in big costs and the college loses the ability to explore more productive teaching techniques.
- Tenure inhibits the flexibility of colleges to move teachers around to more relevant and in-demand fields.
- Tenured professors don't have to change how they teach to fit the advancing technology and changing student demographics.
- Tenured positions can more effectively be replaced by contracts (similar to the business world) that could be removed if the professor does not perform well.

There is quite a wide range of responses to these points. Recessions have shown that tenure does not protect people when the college simply erases the position or, as happens more regularly than it might seem, the entire department that contained the position. As for the third point, the United States has long been considered a source of higher education admired around the world, particularly its graduate education.

Skipping through to the last point, one- or two-year contracts do not give enough job security or ability for professors to apply for long-term grants, so, most research-focused institutions are not going to eliminate the tenure system anytime soon. This may benefit you as a potential part-time person who is interested in teaching a course and not in a tenure track, because those institution's researchers will be more focused on grants and research, with reduced teaching loads compared to other faculty. Yet courses still need to be taught and that is where you come in.

Now that we have some of the biggest points out of the way, we'll focus the rest of this chapter summarizing some of the title terminology you will come across in academia, particularly among the professoriate. From the outside it may seem like everyone is equal, but clearly there is a hierarchy, and some are more equal than others.

Faculty Levels and Roles

Adjunct Faculty

That's you! Adjuncts are faculty members who are part-time university employees; they are typically paid by the course and can teach one or more courses on a semester-by-semester basis. Each course taught will usually trigger a new contract. Many institutions have started placing limits on the number of courses you are allowed to teach per semester (and year) to avoid the appearance of you being a full-time employee.

Within an academic department, an adjunct lecturer's sole responsibility is to teach their classes. They have no voting authority and are not expected and probably prohibited from participating in department or university governance. If a university's faculty have unionized, it is possible that there may be a contingent faculty labor organization as well, in which case there may be some opportunity for labor-related governance activities. However, each department is semiautonomous when it comes to departmental self-governance and can potentially offer some additional responsibility to an adjunct, but it will not be explicitly written into a contract. Beware, any additional responsibility will be essentially volunteer service.

The title of adjunct can also be used in conjunction with the titles of professor, instructor, or lecturer depending mainly on your terminal degree. Academia is a status game and a PhD being hired as an adjunct may negotiate the title of adjunct professor over adjunct lecturer. However, the approval in granting a contingent position may limit the flexibility of the offerer on what can be negotiated.

Adjunct Assistant Research Professor

Now that's a mouthful. That was the title that I (Daniel) was conferred upon starting my second academic gig. I had recently finished grad school, working on a NASA fellowship, and the family decided to move to New England. I was the trailing spouse to a medical doctor (the most useful kind of doctor) and pitched my services to local universities. Having been warned by my NASA colleagues to avoid academia at all costs, I decided that an adjunct position would be all I would seek out while trying to keep up with my scholarly pursuits. To be recognized by the university I drew interest from, I was required to teach at least one class per semester, which, in the beginning, I happily did. I later came to find that to be able to lead federally funded research, I would have to be employed in a full-time position, which began my bizarre 14-year stint as a professor in higher ed. In hindsight, I think my NASA colleagues were mostly right. If I had to do it again, I would have just stuck to being an adjunct while pursuing full-time or entrepreneurial work. Going back to my title, adjunct can be slapped in front of just about any rank and title in higher education.

Lecturers/Instructors

This could be you. Most adjuncts are adjunct lecturer or instructor by title, but lecturer is a more general category. Lecturers and Instructors are terms often used interchangeably, but are hierarchical in some systems. Graduate students who are employed in a College's Writing Program might have the title of writing instructor, for example.

Lecturers can be temporary or permanent full-time employees hired to teach several courses per academic year. It is not uncommon for a lecturer to teach anywhere from 6 to 10 courses per academic year, or 3 to 5 per semester. These are commonly referred to by "load" so three courses taught each semester would be called a 3–3 load. Courses can be measured by individual classes for which material is prepared and presented or measured by contact time with the students. Accordingly, not all courses are equal. For example, a 3-credit-hour lecture course may count the same as a 1.5-credit-hour laboratory course when it comes to tallying the lecturer's teaching count.

As with adjunct contracts, many institutions will limit the number of consecutive years an individual can be hired as a full-time lecturer. Many university tenure and promotion policies will consider a faculty member regardless of title to be "vested" with a de facto tenure once they work for six or seven consecutive years. Universities have taken to using the term "temporary, full-time" to ensure a legal understanding that despite being full-time with the ability to collect benefits, these employees are contingent. The more common approach is to continue such lecturers on a part-time basis, so they do not become vested as full-time employees. At some state schools part-time lecturers also have certain vested rights as well, but prorated or not to the same degree as full timers.

Loads Keep Rising

Most older, likely tenured faculty, especially professors, scoff at the idea of teaching more than two to three courses per semester. But as time has gone on, universities are pushing the limits of what a lecturer may be willing to accept for a full teaching load (Marcus 2021a). What used to be a standard 4–4 teaching load for faculty at four-year institutions (3–3 teaching load for faculty at the assistant professor or higher rank) has been growing to include anywhere from one to two extra classes per semester. Both 4–3 and 4–4 loads are becoming more common for professors and some institutions are trying to push for 5–5 loads on lecturers. Two-year colleges frequently have 4–4 loads for professors. As these types of institutions are often the main competitors for four-year schools seeking entering students, their increased cost savings as a result of this higher teaching load is a source of interest for four-year college administrators.

Lecturers do not need to have terminal degrees, and many are hired on for their specific expertise. However, as the PhD market continues to be saturated in practically every field of study, university departments can become more discriminating to candidates with doctoral degrees. You will find plenty of full-time and part-time lecturers with doctorates. (They are primarily compared with other lecturers on the basis of how willingly and how well they teach.) Lecturers can also obtain the rank of senior lecturer, indicating more experience and higher rank (remember, status game), which often allows for a higher pay.

"Regular" lecturers and instructors tend to have more security than adjuncts because if a course gets canceled and the lecturer/instructor is full time or on a permanent part-time position, they will get moved to teaching another class or perhaps get an alternative assignment. Contingent faculty do not have that security. If a course gets canceled, they lose their contract and job for that class.

Professor, Professor, and Professor

There are three ranks commonly associated with the title of professor: assistant, associate, and full—typically just labeled *professor*. These are permanent, full-time positions and professors at four-year institutions almost always hold a terminal degree of PhD or equivalent. Professors at two-year institutions almost always hold a master's degree, although PhDs are highly sought. The positions typically operate under annual, 9-month (sometimes 10-month) contracts, with an expectation for teaching, scholarship, and service during those contract months. The off-contract time happens in the summer, and it is understood that faculty will pursue uninterrupted scholarship during that time. Assistant professors typically adhere to this understanding because they want to receive tenure, while associate and full professors are more likely to be tempted by gardening or golf in between working on their unpublished manuscripts. Thus, the summers may seem quite deserted with faculty absent unless they have a research grant or some weird work obsession/compulsion that requires a laboratory or a library.

While professorships are typically permanent, full-time positions, they may follow either a tenure or nontenure track. Regardless, tenure and nontenure track positions follow nearly identical standards for promotion. Tenure and promotion usually follow an annual evaluation process over the course of 6 to 10 years, which requires the documentation of achievements in scholarship, teaching, and service. Professor often means tenure-track, and again the hierarchy is assistant, associate, and full—the latter two being conferred upon promotion.

As with most of the titles you find in academia, the title of professor can be modified in several ways. Research professors focus solely on research with little or no classroom teaching responsibility, but possibly graduate student mentorship. These positions are usually funded by grants or "soft" money and often end when the grant funding terminates. Teaching professors focus solely on teaching, but are also typically intimately involved in curriculum development for their department and they often also conduct scholarly research in pedagogy. These can be tenure- or nontenure-track positions. Clinical professors and professors of practice focus on teaching from practical expertise.

A university or college may have an even higher level such as "distinguished professor" not normally reached. Tenure-track positions generally include teaching fewer courses than lecturers, but additionally include research and service expectations, and the opportunity to apply for sabbaticals. The title has consequences outside the university. Some federal-level grant opportunities require the principal investigator (PI) to be among the professorial ranks, rather than lecturer or instructor.

Emeritus/Emerita faculty

You might see an older person hanging around but not teaching. Retired faculty sometimes receive the designation of emeritus if they are male, or emerita if they are female (plural is "emeriti"—academia still loves to use Latin). So, designated faculty retain privileges that may include an office, participation in university functions, and the ever coveted ".edu" email address. They are reliable sources of university wisdom and connection. They are good people to ask questions of and seek advice as you begin and continue your adjunct life.

Visiting Professors

Visiting professors represent short-term, full-time faculty positions. Historically, there have been two main types of visiting professors. The first type are those who take a leave of absence in the form of a sabbatical from their home institution. This magical sabbatical year off (now typically just one semester, as many institutions save money by offering either a fully salaried single semester or half-salaried two semesters), originally instituted by Harvard in 1880, allows for undisturbed career replenishment after six years (typically) of continuous university employment paralleling the Sabbath day of rest in Judeo-Christian religions (Eells 1962). During this period, a professor might learn new skills and techniques sometimes in a faraway country, perhaps finish long put off papers or books, or start an entirely new research program. It is common for faculty on sabbatical to visit other institutions as part of their sabbatical work. Sometimes such connections can lead to a scenario in which they perform an exchange or substitution for a semester or year, receiving a title of visiting professor.

The second type of visiting professor, on the other hand, is typically extended to early-career PhDs on an annual basis, sometimes renewable up to three years. These contracts are fixed and often have a singular focus on teaching. There are typically few, if any, opportunities for visiting professors to collaborate on research; however, these contract faculty are encouraged to work on their own research project once their teaching duties are satisfied. This contract professor is often employed as a temporary stop gap for a faculty member who is on sick leave or who is on sabbatical. (Who said substitute teachers were only for grade school?) Universities typically allocate these positions to novices not only to provide valued experience but also to maximize cost savings for an assistant or associate professor. Visiting professors often teach more than the associate or full professor they are temporarily replacing. Just as it is foolhardy to imagine an adjunct position being transformed into a tenured position, it is equally foolhardy to imagine visiting appointments to do the same (Devereaux 2024). Academic job searches for new faculty almost invariably look for freshly minted PhDs that come from stellar pedigrees. Variations from this are likely only due to shifting market forces or geography.

"Ranking" Titles

Lecturer is considered lower ranked than a tenured professor. Tenured is respected in the academic community and some people don't see lecturers or nontenured professors as deserving the same respect, especially in the United States. Again, this is often of little import to the student and everyone else outside of academia, who simply see someone who teaches in higher education as a "professor" or particularly among new freshmen as "teacher." Most faculty don't really care if someone else has a Lecturer or Instructor title either. They only care that courses are being taught and that they themselves don't have to do the teaching. But, if given a choice, the majority of university faculty would prefer the title of Professor. (There are other implications of being a professor rather than a lecturer that we need not go into here, such as the ability to apply for federal grant funding.)

Despite this sometimes ludicrous deference to rank and title in higher education, the majority of college courses are taught by faculty who are part-time or do not have tenure. This is good news for potential contingent faculty, but there are some implications to be aware of. Colleges and universities do not typically invest in contingent faculty; certainly not to the extent they do with "regular" faculty. But academic institutions know they depend on contingent faculty to deliver the curricula. Full- or part-time, lecturer or instructor, or professor—generally this makes no difference in what must be done to prepare for and teach a course. Books must be ordered, syllabi written, guest speakers scheduled, lectures to be taught, committee assignments dodged, and papers to be graded.

Administrative Leadership

Administrative ranks are hierarchical positions such as department chair, assistant dean, associate dean, dean, director, assistant provost, associate provost, provost, president, and other titles. Academic rank usually refers to the lecturer/instructor and professorial ranks. An administrator might not have an academic professorial rank, or they might have negotiated such upon their hiring. In the latter case, they can "retreat" to it after their deanship or other administrative service is concluded. Dual appointment is particularly useful for promotion within the ranks, as a professor is unlikely to want to surrender tenure for a relatively short-term administrative appointment.

At first this can seem confusing as, for example, an associate professor can be a dean, overseeing departments with full professors. Some departments have assistant professors or even instructors as department chairs (either there are no senior faculty or, more likely, the senior faculty have all figured out how to wiggle out of this responsibility and the college lets them).

The line is blurred between teaching faculty and faculty who hold dual administrative positions. To add to the confusion, deans, directors, provosts, and even presidents may also teach a class or two. A good way to think of it is everyone is there to help students learn and everyone is an educator. The lower administrative leadership positions, particularly associate deans, may be dual appointments held by someone who is also a faculty member. A faculty member may also be in charge of the institution's Center for Teaching, typically with one or more course-releases as an additional benefit. The heads of other student support offices, student advising services, technical services related to teaching, and other offices will generally be full-time administrative staff who are not faculty, although as we've said, they may teach a course from time to time.

A large department may have assistant or associate chairs and heads of majors or programs within the department. There may also be a curriculum coordinator within the department, who will also be a full-time faculty member and a person you as an adjunct would likely be in contact with if there are concerns aligning your course within the course sequences of the department. Beyond the level of department head, you will not likely have much involvement unless, and we don't mean to scare you off, some student grievance or discipline issues arise.

Generally speaking, the faculty "owns" the curriculum (i.e., they get to create and deliver it, without intervention from above) and the role of the higher-ups is to deal with everything else. The president is largely responsible for political and policy aspects of the institution. The provost handles the academic side of things, which means supervising the deans, who in turn leave it to the department heads. So it takes a while to get things done. Again, your memories of how things were as where you pursued your own education will largely suffice because there is almost a protective cap around adjuncts in terms of being affected by policy and university-level concerns. You will be focused on honoring your contract by delivering your course. But here is a reminder and possibly an update about deans and provosts—the most important academic administrators in terms of your job as an adjunct.

The Department Chair: Heartbeat of the Department

Other than the students themselves, the department chair position is the most critical at the university. There is a good chance that only the department chair thinks this is true. However, approximately 80 percent of academic decisions are made at the department level, although they may be collective and endorsed, or officially issued at a higher level— usually dean or associate dean. Only about 3 percent of chairs receive training in leadership. As Gmelch writes, "academic leadership is one of the few professions one can enter today with absolutely no training" (Gmelch 2015, 1–2). This means faculty members must be particularly alert to what is going on especially in case the chair is not.

Most chairs see themselves as faculty and virtually all still teach. This is good because chairs in many institutions rotate back to the rank-and-file in about six or so years, unless the dean and their colleagues can bully them into remaining longer. In other institutions the chair is a manager rather than a professor and continues as such indefinitely, with little teaching.

Gmelch (2015) summarizes the four main roles of department chairs:

- Faculty developer
- Manager (often a least favorite part of the job)

- Leader (as chief advocates for academic programs and academic disciplines)
- Scholar (chairs have to keep afloat as scholar-teachers while acting as chief administrators for their academic units/disciplines)

For the adjunct and other faculty members, the chair is the chief point of contact for everything from curriculum to office space. A good dean recognizes the key role of chairs and generally supports their positions on personnel, curriculum, and other matters.

A Possible Warning Sign

Some senior faculty avoid serving as chairs because of the frustration of added responsibility coupled with little authority and a poor operating budget. You might recognize this possibility if you see a department loaded with associate and full professors but having a lecturer as chair. They might be grooming him or her for leadership and advancement, but on the other hand it could just be either the institution is starved for resources or does not use best leadership management practices. When you are considering an adjunct position, pay attention to who chairs the academic department in which you will be teaching because that will give you insight into how the hiring institution views academic leadership and management.

So, remember, department and program chairs are often just members of the faculty who agree to perform this role for a few years. Very few have any formal or informal training in being a chair other than just a half-day seminar or workshop now and then. The implications of this lack of training on departmental decision making and faculty interactions are worth considering in developing a long-term relationship with them as an adjunct. They generally mean well and will be good resources, but will not have all the answers.

Deans: Guardians of Academic Integrity and Budgets

When academics talk about deans, we mean "real" deans—academic deans. Academic deans have to come from the faculty (tenured professor usually at least an associate professor), but other deans such as "Dean of Students" comes from the administration and are seldom "academics" and rarely come in contact with contingent faculty except as student advocates or institutional advocates in matters of student welfare, academic integrity and the like. Academic deans hold an administrative rank that is different from their professorial rank. This means an academic dean might be an associate professor rather than a full professor and might not even hold a professorial rank at all. Historically, academic deans negotiated for a professorial rank (and tenure or shortened tenure track) upon being hired into the position from an external source.

If being promoted (or "penalized," depending on what you think about administrators) from within, the dean candidate will likely already hold a professorial rank. If you are a contingent faculty member, a deanship is probably not in your career arc (nor is it for most tenured faculty either, much to their relief), but you should know who he or she is and what they can do to or for you.

Deans can come from within the institution or are hired to be managers brought in from outside, often to shake things up. Scholarship is a factor in selecting deans, along with management skills. Scholarship must be in there because deans need the respect of their faculty. But faculty do need to be managed. We have seen dean candidates with relatively few management skills, but high publication rates chosen over other dean candidates. Ironically (or not, depending on your view), some of the opposite skills in being a dean are beneficial to scholarship—solitary focus, introversion, single-mindedness. Hmm, on second thought, maybe they are helpful in being a dean too.

Deans like to have assistant or associate deans. Associate deans carry out what the deans want to do (the enforcers if they actually have power, gofers if they do not) and have a wide range of responsibilities all around the university administration (including budget recommendations, oversee staff and/or faculty, increase university retention and enrollment, solving administrative problems, and making solutions happen). The associate dean's title might represent their key role, as in Associate Dean for Research or Associate Dean for Teaching and Learning.

Deans coordinate with the various offices around the university and with the board of visitors and other community members. They are the face of the college or school to the community. They have to show up at various academic and public events. They are also sometimes measured by their ability to fundraise, which can be crucial to keep STEM-related disciplines well-funded and up to date technically.

Lastly, a dean is a buffer between the academic department and the provost. It is a dean's job to wheedle, extort, delegate, and deny funding requests. A dean approves academic appointments, although it is likely the higher-ups also have to approve things but mostly, they take their cue from the dean. A dean will likely be the one to sign contingent faculty contracts, but it is quite likely the dean will not know who the contingent faculty is; that knowledge is the job of the department head.

Provosts: The Chief Academic Officer

A provost we know likes to preface talks with the question, "What is a Provost?" She started out doing it rhetorically, but quickly found out many people have no idea what a provost actually is. Some might think it is the chief academic officer (CAO), but provosts often also have the title "Vice President for Academic Affairs," which sounds like the same thing.

Usually, it means the rank below college or university president that heads up the academic side of things. By now, you probably have a good idea of how muddy academic terminology can be. Deans report to the provost. As an adjunct you are not likely to see the provost except perhaps from a distance at a cocktail party (that you weren't invited to), but this is the person who is in charge of college administrative structure and academic programs, so they are important in allowing the department to hire adjuncts. Of course, the department chair will do the actual work, but the provost will guard the budget. This can range from tuition, whether course enrollments are sufficient to let a course run, lab fees, and other financial aspects related to delivery of the curriculum. This is not to be confused (or perhaps it is) with the chief financial officer (CFO), with whom you are much more likely to be familiar if you are coming from the private professional sector.

The provost oversees a great many things that have to do with the curriculum, but the curriculum usually "belongs" to the faculty. This is often a source of frustration to the provost. However, the true job of a provost, as told to us by John Hegarty, provost of Trinity College Dublin (December 18, 2003), is to hire faculty who are "smarter and better scholars than me" and clear obstacles out of their way. As long as it is within budget, of course.

Is the Provost Responsible for the Curriculum?

As CAO, the provost is technically responsible for the curriculum. However, the faculty in the department provide a curriculum that meets expectations for the granting of a degree in the proscribed field. The departments conduct self-studies that circulate for peer and external review and make recommendations for all aspects, including curriculum. Regionally based accrediting bodies conduct periodic reviews to see if standards are met, as do various professional bodies (such as the Accreditation Board for Engineering and Technology, ABET; or the Council for the Accreditation of Educator Preparation, CAEP; there are many others, particularly for STEM fields). Departments also undergo periodic peer reviews from external committees with expertise in the department's fields of study. These all inform (and protect) curriculum offerings. In many ways, the provost has the final say because resources are what make the curriculum operational.

As is the case with deans, provosts can proliferate and the institution may have associate or assistant provosts in various subcategories within academia, such as "vice provost for graduate education" or "associate provost for community engagement." Most places now have some kind of associate or vice provost for diversity and inclusion.

Finally, some institutions are more "stable" than others—the unstable ones often experience frequent churn up the higher ranks. This means that provost and dean positions will change and with them, the priorities of the university. Especially for provosts that take on the job as a stepping stone up to the next, more prestigious higher ed position, they will attempt to make significant changes to either core curriculum, programmatic offerings, or the makeup of departments and types of faculty (more researchers versus teachers or vice versa). While these are most often done with good intentions, these activities serve an added benefit of enhancing an administrator's CV (curriculum vitae, a long version of a resume, used primarily by academics) for the next job they are already looking for. It's just the nature of higher ed, and very minimally a concern of contingent faculty.

The Myth, the Legend, the University President

While the provost is the CAO of a college or university, the president is the CEO. According to Gwynedd Mercy University (2024), university presidents enact the decisions of the university's board of trustees and assign and delegate goals and tasks to the other administrators at the university. They ideally provide vision and leadership for the institution and meet frequently with local leaders, donors, and policy makers, as well as the university community, including students, staff, and faculty to highlight, carry out, and gain support for their established goals. They meet frequently with their provosts, deans, and administrative staff to delegate responsibilities for carrying out their mission.

From our experience, university presidents are mostly figureheads for the institution when the board of trustees (and/or chancellor in a state university system) want the status quo, and they are idolized and celebrated during good times while demonized and scrutinized during bad times. At stable (read well-funded) universities, presidents have the freedom to develop a comprehensive strategic plan for the institution, with the standard vision, mission, goals, objectives, and priorities that adorn university websites. And they actually take steps to implement this plan. At institutions in crisis and turmoil, they are often given leeway in making decisions that are hoped to right the proverbial ship that has gone astray from the mission. However, this may result in zig-zagging of the direction the institution takes when rapid turnover of leadership ensues. Forward motion when zig-zagging is hard to detect.

Unless scheduled and announced, presidential sightings are akin to bald eagle sightings. Rare but exciting when it happens. Well, less exciting than a bald eagle sighting, obviously, but making about the same difference to how you carry out your responsibilities as contingent faculty. Some presidents at small- to moderate-sized institutions make it a point to meet as many faculty as possible, including contingent ones, and will be quite good at remembering names. So hide your shock if this happens to you, although it is permitted and even advisable to look suitably impressed. At the heart of any good president is a faculty member who cares about teaching, and the role of contingent faculty such as you.

The Role of Nonacademic Staff

We mentioned earlier that there are many administrative and support staff who go into carrying out an institution's mission and into providing quality education to students. From janitorial staff to custodians to security, there are several essential services that universities and colleges must invest in. It's always a best practice to be courteous with these folks. Beyond it just being the decent thing to do, these staffers are likely going to be able to let you into a locked classroom after hours, move you to another room if one is occupied by a professor who refuses to leave, and they'll help you arrange for a tow truck when your car breaks down.

As far as administrative staff goes, again, the department AA is the one person you need to know well and be good friends with. They will make your life very nice or they will have you wishing you got off to a better start with them. Find out their birthday and sign the card. Buy them a coffee from time to time. Take time to listen to them. You will find that they know the students, the institution, and the faculty as well if not better than anyone. Likely also, this knowledge is couched in the pragmatic sense that will be useful to you: who does what and how efficiently they do it (and how best to get along with them). As departments continue to shrink, AAs can be assigned multiple departments and take an increasingly important role as your connection to department culture, students, and other faculty.

Lastly, at least at our most recent stints as full-time professors, the administrative leadership decided to move student advising, especially in the first years of attending, away from being strictly done by faculty. A new layer of professional academic advisers was hired to help take the load off for faculty, sparing them from helping students fill out their course schedules so that the faculty are able to focus more on curriculum and teaching. The logic of doing this is sound for very large major departments such as business and biology, where many students plan to graduate with a degree in these subjects. Although it distances faculty from their students. For small departments, it can be challenging because the curriculum may be a little bit more nuanced or fluid. You might feel this shouldn't impact contingent faculty much. But more and more, students are entering academia with less preparation, more stress, and in greater need of advising and related services.

You may find a student ends up in your class without the proper prerequisites to take your course, or perhaps meets the prerequisites but lacks the necessary skills for success or has the skillset but needs to be shown how to use it. Or, you may find a connection you have made with a student leads them to confide in you about their academic progress and career plans and you want to be able to reassure them about what structures exist to support them. Be sure to determine if the institution uses professional advisers, faculty advisers, or some combination of both. For example, some institutions assign freshmen a professional adviser and shift to a faculty adviser once the student chooses a major or enters their junior year.

Conclusion

Academia has its own terminology. Knowing the rankings of faculty positions and how they are defined can be useful in negotiations and in seeing how your adjunct position "fits" in the institution. Your background and education may qualify you for a higher position than offered, but the positional rank may be predetermined and not negotiable. In such cases, you may have an opportunity for an increase in rank and, potentially, pay in subsequent contracts.

As an adjunct you are not going to be in a tenure track position, but it is helpful to know what that is. Particularly because tenure is a major factor at many institutions. And there is frequent tension around the issue of tenure. Some institutions even use adjunct positions to weaken the case for tenure in general. Fortunately, if you are contemplating a position at an institution with this sort of dynamic, it will probably already have manifested itself publicly in the media and you can be forewarned. Regardless, if you are interested in an academic career beyond being an adjunct, it is useful to know what constitutes full time permanent positions.

The courses you teach as an adjunct are part of the curriculum, which is set by the faculty. Each academic department determines its own curriculum, which is then approved by the faculty as a whole. If the course is in an academic department, and the "regular" faculty are not available to teach it, then that department's chair will usually be the lead in a search to recruit an adjunct to teach it. Courses in special programs such as Honors follow a similar route, although the faculty will represent multiple academic disciplines, with searches being undertaken by the program director. A further category of courses might be specific to "general education" and not subject to a particular department or program, but again they will be under the auspices of a group of faculty. Accordingly, in most cases, your hiring begins with a faculty committee of some sort, after you clear the HR minimum position requirements, and then proceeds to approval by an administrator, usually a director if it is in a special program or dean if it is a regular department course or position.

Academia has two parallel sets of structure in its personnel. It has the academic faculty, and it has the supporting structure of administrators and services. Administrators fall into two camps, support services, and those directly in the academic hierarchy, beginning with chairs and directors (who may or may not be "managers" but who most certainly do most of the managing), to assistant deans, associate deans, deans, and on through provosts to the president. Support services include the dean of students, and anything from advising students, to residential assistants, libraries, technical support, and many other things designed to improve student lives and their learning.

As an adjunct you are a member of the academic faculty and should have the same privileges as other faculty regarding any teaching support services such as library, computer lab, and technical services. You also need to have some sense of the student support services so you can steer students to them as you deem appropriate. You may find opportunities to attend faculty training helpful although as an adjunct you are not as likely to have the time for such things. But much can be done via online or by arranging meetings before or after your teaching slot on campus. Your department chair and department administrative assistant are likely the best link to administrative services and support.

CHAPTER 3

Understanding the Students

Students in a Continuum of Learning

We are all familiar with the freshman, sophomore, junior, and senior sequences. Even if we hadn't experienced it firsthand in college, we would be aware of it from high school, which follows a parallel sequence. We also know it well from TV and film; academia and college life are ripe ground for harvesting comedic and dramatic stories.

However, also from experience we know that institutions use a credit-achieved basis for determining academic standing rather than what actual year they are in. We used to divide students based on the traditional sequence, assuming a continual progression from kindergarten to four-year college graduate (K-16) without interruption, and nontraditional, which breaks from this tradition. But the distinction between traditional and nontraditional has gradually lost much context with so many students earning advanced placement (AP) or "early college" credit before ever stepping foot on campus and others following different pathways as lifelong learners. In a rare move to simplify things, we just call them students—or "learners" if we are trying to sound enlightened.

Beyond the more commonly encountered nontraditional learner sequence, new adjuncts who have been out of college for a while may benefit from a summary of what the students are like these days. For the rest of us these terms may be a helpful reminder, plus it is important to see how the graduation rates have changed and how much education has become a part-time pursuit. We truly are becoming a nation of lifelong learners.

Navigating the Four-Year Sequence

The four-year sequence is most likely to be followed at residential private colleges and universities. It is still common and for the most part followed at public research institutions as well; however, you are much more likely to find nontraditional students at public, regional comprehensive universities and at most community colleges. The majority of learners completing coursework to earn a degree today will graduate from the latter two institutions. Further, pursuit of the four-year sequence is quite likely to take six years rather than four.

For learners who follow the traditional sequence straight out of high school, it will be marked by the entry into adulthood and the assumptions of increased responsibility and independence. FERPA, the Family Educational Rights and Privacy Act (20 USC § 1232g; 34 CFR Part 99), continues to protect their academic privacy, but now they are usually 18 or older and legally adults. The excitement and apprehension of the first year includes adjusting to college life, adjusting to a new-found independence, and waking up to the fact that school—what was once a common commodity to be taken for granted like air and water—is now something that someone has to pay for directly. It can take a while to learn that. Additionally, there is often new academic rigor.

Students are now in class about half as long as in high school, but cover material twice as fast. Courses that were a year in high school are now a semester. Seat time is halved but knowledge responsibilities are doubled. Students have professors not teachers, which means the presumption is they already know how to learn and just need someone to "profess" to them. They must learn "academic self-management." They also must learn how to get along with roommates and other outside-the-home adjustments if they are not commuters. If you are teaching a freshman course, particularly a first semester course, you may find it useful to remind your students of some of these differences. You may also find it useful that many students have yet to know how to learn and budget their time.

Students may take a while to realize they are in a job, the job of being a student. If done to maximize the chances of earning an "A," it is a full-time job. The 15 credits per semester required to complete a 60-credit associates degree in 2 years or a 120-credit bachelor degree in 4 years assumes 15 hours of in-class time per week plus 25 hours of homework/studying per week, adding up to a 40-hour work week, regardless of whether they have other jobs. It may take students a few semesters or more to internalize this information. The increasing cost of education is making it ever more important for students to be pragmatic in approaching the "job" of a student as an investment.

Six-Year Graduation Rates, Not Four

The typical graduation sequence is much more likely to be six years or more, according to the National Center for Educational Statistics (2024). Yet 90 percent of Baccalaureate students expect to get their degree in four years (Marcus 2021b). Many college students do not internalize the fact that 15 credits per semester add up to 30 per year and that times 4 equals the 120-credit minimum for a bachelor's degree. But that alone is not enough to explain why it often takes more than four years to get a BA or BS. Between unexpected health issues (by the student or close family), dropping a class that is only offered every two years, double majoring, or picking up a part- or full-time job during school, there are many unplanned and unintentional events that impact the actual time to graduate.

By their second-year sophomores navigate declaring their major of study, expand networks, and deepen academic engagement. In their junior year they have had the basics of their majors, progressed through much of general education requirements, and begun specializations. They are balancing academic responsibilities with internships, research, and extracurricular activities. Through the senior year they continue to specialize and prepare for their careers. Some signs of stress may appear as they realize (we hope) the need to plan for graduation and the transition to postcollege life. The final semester of the senior year sees the culmination of academic projects (sometimes in formal capstone courses), job searches, reflections on the college experience, and the development of nascent professional connections.

Diverse Student Profiles on the Rise

What we used to think of as "nontraditional students" are returning learners, part-time students, and those juggling work or family commitments. You may also have international students who are navigating cultural transitions and academic expectations, often in a non-native language. There are other groupings of students. Some generational differences may exist. Clearly, students are individual learners but perhaps there are some common tendencies we may see based on how we group our students.

Understanding Different Generations

Generalizing about students from a particular generation carries risks of imparting judgment and bias. However, from the perspective of structuring best learning practices, some generalizations may be helpful, particularly if the instructor is from a different generation. "Millennials" are not the current group of traditional college-aged learners—who belong to "Generation Z"—but they share many characteristics. Also, we address Millennials as comprising a significant portion of contingent faculty—a source of wonder and vexation for "Generation X" professors and aging "Baby Boomer" department chairs. (Much to their chagrin, Millennials are largely the children of Baby Boomers and Generation X.) Millennials can be defined in different birth ranges; 1981 to 1996 or 1997 is typical. Generation Z is from about 1996 or 1997. Well this is getting fuzzy again, let's go with the Pew Research Center's definitions (Dimock 2019) and wait for more data to go beyond Generation Z (Generation Alpha?).

- The Silent Generation: Born 1928 to 1945
- Baby Boomers: Born 1946 to 1964
- Generation X: Born 1965 to 1980
- Millennials: Born 1981 to 1996

- Generation Z: Born 1997 to 2012

Much of this section reflects *Teaching at its Best*, by Neilson (2010). Let's start with Millennials. This group may comprise a significant portion of your nontraditional learners. The direct nature of Millennials means teachers have to dress the part. This is especially important if students are older than the teacher (not a problem for some of us). The teacher needs to look professional so the students will take the teacher seriously and think they are getting their money's worth. For those of us in the applied fields, especially field sciences, do not worry about having to dress formally. Professional is different, it means you can wear jeans if you are going out to sample insects, for example. A good rule of thumb is to dress as you would in a professional setting of the degree most closely related to the subject you are teaching. If you are reading this as an adjunct or an adjunct-to-be, it means you won't have to change clothes to go teach your course.

Millennial learners want applied learning. They do not typically learn things just to learn them (as intrinsically motivated learners would). They want to know what the knowledge is used for and they need outside (extrinsic) motivation. This is quite a change for many baby boomers, who learned things simply because someone was teaching them. Millennials want to see the connection between what is learned in the classroom and the real world. In this way, Millennials are similar to engineers and other applied professions even if they are in theoretical fields. This can make things interesting, and it comports with a transactional view of education.

Astonishingly to Baby Boomers and what remains of their seniors from the Greatest Generation, some Millennial learners never lived in a world without new technology (iPhones, computers, cars with onboard navigational and operational systems, and so forth). Teaching Millennials and subsequent generations creates an interesting challenge for professors. Some factors to consider:

- Instructors need to navigate how to use the ever-advancing technology in a way that is engaging and productive.

- There will be pressure to use said technology or students are going to leave and find a teacher that will (they won't be connected to the material if technology doesn't match what they're used to).
- You might need to change or mix in various teaching techniques. The "generational divide" means you might have to move away from traditional podium lectures, or at least supplement with other practices.
- Millennials expect things faster. They want instant responses, follow-ups, services, and so on.
- Millennials expect to be engaged in learning. They are not passive learners, even though they will (happily) passively stream shows on their phones.
- Many are extrinsically motivated learners. This ties in with loss of attention span due access to multiple digital stimuli.

Generation Z is more ethnically diverse than previous generations and more likely to have a parent who has gone to college. For Millennials and more recent generations, learning more closely follows gaming methods rather than logic. Gaming is trial and error repetition. Since games have rules, Millennials and Generation Z can handle structure fairly well. Losing a game represents learning (trial and error). However, trial and error is not the best approach for deep learning. We sometimes need to think about the fundamental process of something to more fully understand it.

Millennial and Generation Z student attributes (from Northern Illinois University Center for Innovative Teaching and Learning 2020) will affect how they learn and how you can best reach them. Some considerations are as follows:

- Computers are not just technology for Millennials, they have entirely become an aspect of their life.
- Reality is no longer real. Simulations, teleconference, emails not necessarily coming from the address, altered images, and so on, all have been normalized for this generation.
- Doing is more important than knowing.

- Because facts are so easily obtained, learning facts is not viewed as important.
- "Multitasking" is a way of life. Students do multiple things at the same time, such as listening to music and texting while studying. This can be distracting because the brain needs to focus on one thing at a time, but younger generations believe they can buck biological realities.
- They have no easy tolerance for delays. They expect immediate responses to their queries and revolt with even short grading delays.
- Creator, owner, and consumer distinctions are blurred. Once something is out on the internet, it is common knowledge and "cut and paste" is okay—it belongs to all. Citations for referencing and attribution accountability is a problem.
- They expect and are comfortable with classes and lectures that are multimedia and multimodal. This means you could develop and offer multiple learning pathways. For example, people who choose not to participate in class discussion could instead be active in an online chat or a Zoom breakout room.
- They will want to use a pdf version of any textbook you require, because they likely downloaded an illegal copy so as not to pay for it (see the previous bullet point on creator, owner, and consumer distinctions). If you require a physical copy to use it in class, you will be inviting the use of laptops and tablets, if not an outright revolt.

There is also something important to realize with current students. They aren't as tech savvy as many profess them to be. Sure, they can use a device and maneuver an app, but do not expect them to easily set up a pivot table in Microsoft Excel or have them fix your faulty projector connection in the classroom. Their skill is in being fluent users of technology where they can do rudimentary google searches and easily navigate user interfaces. To use software as actual tools still requires concentration and effort, which bodes well for the older teaching generation.

Generation Z

Generation Z continues the trends manifested in Millennials. In class, Generation Z has spent more time on standardized state-level competency tests than previous generations. Thus, they may need a boost in using more creative learning assessments. Indeed, to keep up with mandates, K-12 schools have deemphasized creative approaches and imaginative learning (see Miller and Grace 2016, 177). A little over half of the states do not require writing in cursive for current K-12 students, which may be quite shocking to those of us in previous generational groups. In compensation, such students may be more adept at using computer tablets in the classroom. Nevertheless, these students may have difficulty reading faculty handwriting on the board, or reading historical handwritten documents (Northern Illinois University 2020).

Generation Z does not use email daily, so if that is your preferred method of communicating you will have to make sure they are aware of it and use it, as their own inclination will be to text you. You probably do not want to be texted by all (or any) of your classes, or it will threaten to take over your life.

Essentially, whether it is Millennials and Generation Z's mythical "learning styles" (see Chapter 6) and relationship to technology, academic survival as an adjunct, or "regular" faculty for that matter, means adapt and incorporate or get left behind.

Students as Consumers

> Academia is the only industry where the customer complains when they receive too much product for their money.

Many students now view higher education as a high-priced consumer transaction, so when they don't do well they blame it on the professor not doing their job. From this perspective, the professor is not seen as a professor anymore, they are seen as an overpaid customer service representative. The consumer model is not a true representation of public schooling, where education is usually subsidized.

In public education, and largely in private education, the customer is not the student, the customer is the community (i.e., taxpayers, alumni donors, etc.). This reflects the social contract of the academy. As an adjunct you are participating in the delivery of this social contract, mostly for free. These days, the contract in part includes delivering what the business community wants, which is basic literacy and functionality. As the title of journalist Martha White's article states, "Companies want tech skills and the ability to write in complete sentences" (White 2017). Many students (or their parents) choose elective courses based on these criteria.

The Millennial and Generation Z learners are particularly attuned to the consumer model, as are people coming back to school after having experience in the workforce. College education is applied learning, an economic good they access as consumers. Under this paradigm, education is a commodity and a right, not a privilege (Neilson 2010). An adjunct hired to come in and teach a course as a professional from the field is particularly appropriate for meeting this transactional perspective. Of course, because so much of learning occurs outside the classroom, and for other reasons, the consumer model is usually not sufficient to capture the total college experience for the student. In this model, contingent professors are brought in to deliver a product to students along with the regular faculty. Usually, this means more contingent faculty than regular faculty but let's look at what happens in a consumer approach.

A UK Perspective

Bunce, Baird, and Jones (2016) examined how a UK approach to students by treating them as consumers affected learner identity and performance. Among the results is an indication that a higher consumer orientation in students (i.e., the more a student thinks of themself as a consumer in higher education) suggests lower academic performance. A consumer approach tends to reinforce a degree attitude that doing the minimum will still get you the degree and the job in the end because you are "buying" the degree. The researchers also found that a clearly identified or highly defined job outcome tends to match with a consumer approach to higher education. Unlimited class sizes and no test scores tend to reinforce the idea of students as a consumer. When students pay for school and they're not limited on what they can do, it makes them think they bought it and now own it. This shouldn't be a surprise to you, but it is good to acknowledge it.

Still, the consumer approach does have advantages for the student according to the researchers. There is a palpable shift in power from provider to consumer. Further, the quality of work expected from the professors and other providers of consumer services may rise because the consumer has the economic and social power to demand that the work will fulfill their expectations or demands. In a consumer model, the professors are expected to be available all the time and to respond promptly to students' needs. This approach may be concerning to institutions for several reasons besides that it might make the professors work harder. It might contribute to a conservative status quo mentality. After all, what is there left to learn when you already know it in order to demand it? This certainly poses a risk to academic standards.

Similar to conditions under other models, students will evaluate popular professors more highly than stricter or more "demanding" professors. Popularity ratings can result in pressure for those hard-core, demanding professors to "dumb" down the lectures to get higher ratings (fortunately, the very qualities the best professors possess make them more resistant to such influence). Unfortunately, such pressures may impinge on the learning environment. It may foster a culture where students want a degree more than they want to learn; they might merely seek validation of preexisting knowledge and the credentialing of it in the form of a diploma. This can foster passive attitudes toward learning and reduce desire to produce their own knowledge.

"I Pay His Salary"

We have heard this remark many times during our tenures as professors in academia. It usually gets spewed out in the hallways in between classes by a frustrated student that either didn't receive the grade they thought they deserved or more generally didn't receive an outcome or exception they wanted. The statement is a microcosm of the consumer mentality that exists among many students. Try to resist asking the student to have their accountant calculate the portion of your salary that comes from their tuition or suggesting it be rounded up to a penny so you can refund it. But feel free to think it and to your heart's content.

Getting a Feel for the Local Culture

Contingent professors can figure out the learning environment and culture they want to be a part of by looking for some common themes. Here are four clues provided by Bunce, Baird, and Jones (2016) that you can look for to see if the academic institution or student body engenders a consumer orientation versus a learner orientation:

1. Learner identity
2. Grade as their goal
3. What is their fee responsibility
4. Subject material

"Learner identity" refers to if students identify as a learner or a customer. If the school has mottos, credos, mission statements, and so forth that focus on service and education as an investment, that can be a hint of the commodification of education. Another hint: a learner identity focusing on knowledge, skills, or ability is a good sign that consumerism hasn't quite invaded the culture.

"Grade as their goal" typically points to a college with students on preprofessional tracks such as premedicine and prelaw. Their orientation is going to be driven by how they scored compared to their classmates. These students will often ask, "Is this going to be on the test?" and will definitely be in office hours trying to figure out how you grade assignments and exams, and will be questioning each question you may have marked as incorrect. Getting into medical school or a top law program may depend on a very high GPA for these students, so they will be the most transactional of all of your students.

"What is their fee responsibility" refers to tuition. Fee responsibility is an interesting way to refer to it, but yes, if you pay for a course, you reasonably expect something in return. Perhaps student learning is the real product, and it makes sense to have tangible measurements of that learning. Traditionally, we call this *grades* but students (as customers) might want the thing that grades are supposed to help produce: credentials and jobs. This expectation may be affected by the subject matter; the humanities being notoriously less linked to tangible results compared with, say, engineering or hairdressing.

"Subject material" refers to which subject they are studying. Students who tend to study engineering or nursing will be studying the material because it will result in immediate professional employment in those fields. These subjects attract students who are interested in obtaining training and perhaps licensure to practice in their respective fields.

Turning Consumers Into Professionals

As an incoming adjunct, you may be a long time removed from matters such as classroom behavior, especially if you are not the parent or guardian of school-age children. But it is an important basis for a safe learning environment where the disruption can be about ideas and learning rather than behavior. Rules for speaking, listening, and addressing one another are all valuable parts of classroom etiquette, and are tools for building community. Respect for each other contributes to a positive sense of community. It enables better attention paid in the classroom than might otherwise occur in a disruptive free for all.

Students who address their professors by formal academic title, as opposed to "yo bro," feel like they are getting a better value for their tuition dollar. Rules of etiquette are another thing you can put in the syllabus so you can feel smug when etiquette problems arise and the students claim they were not informed about the rules. However, be careful that you have attended to everything first, like ensuring that your syllabus is accessible to people with learning disabilities, and your course is "digitally compliant" (not that that is clearly defined, but at least your office of student services will have some idea).

Worthen (2017; see also Portwood-Stacer 2016) has sound advice on how to email your professor, and other aspects of good communication. Worthen and Portwood–Stacer note that formal manners and titles aren't elitist; they're meant to ensure respect for everyone. Good communication is part of good classroom etiquette, the goal of which is to enhance student learning. Worthen points out a study that looked at syllabi from 2004 to 2010; 14 percent had a piece about classroom etiquette in 2004. By 2010, that percentage rose to 33 percent. Rules for etiquette are important, especially for online classes. Online classes often have no visual cues on how to act in the setting although we have more and more students brought up in an online learning setting.

A source of etiquette problems arises in the use of cell phones. Phones are great for reading emails, not for writing them. The emails turn out to read like a text not like a professional email from a student–teacher relationship. The writing is not as good. Also, it reinforces students becoming lax and addressing professors by first name rather than title. This is inherently neither good nor bad. Some students need to relax and reduce stress, but too relaxed can impair engagement (and lead to sleep). According to Worthen (2017), encouraging informality goes hand in hand with the informality of social media. Some professors are more comfortable with being called by their first name than others. Same for students. But some might not feel that they are getting their money's worth if they just call an instructor by their first name. For example, at an advanced degree institution, they might ask if you are truly a doctoral-level professor or not. After all, they do not call their physician by a first name.

There are career consequences to informality. Graduates are leaving school with an informal mindset and are mistaking informality for license to act unprofessionally (no one tells you to show up to a meeting and call the boss by their first name when they should be calling them Mr./Ms./They, etc.). Often, the consequences are not direct as in being not chosen for something or left out of a selection process, so a less sensitive person could miss them. A good instructor can show good etiquette means good professional behavior. It does *not* mean no fun.

Student Personality Types

Having accumulated over 50 years of experience and "expert" observation on common behaviors among our students in the classroom, we've come up with a small set of personality types you'll likely encounter and perhaps have to manage. Some of these personality types have stood the test of time, but consequential changes have come about recently with the prevalence of personal technology in the classroom setting. Particularly, students seemingly cannot function without their devices. Laptops, tablets, and smartphones are prevalent in the hallways and in the classrooms. You can fight it, allow it, or embrace it. Whichever way, devices are part of postsecondary classroom culture in the United States.

As you get to know your students, you can find out if they have other factors that are complicating their life and interfering with learning. Know the support structures that can help address this. With that caveat, let's dive into some personalities.

The Distractor/Disruptor Student

The distractor or disruptor student is the student who comes to your class because they think they have a lot to teach the class. They think their opinion is more worthy than yours, sometimes even more worthy than scientific fact, and they'll let you know that. This type of student can really derail class time if you are not careful. The distractor student is semiknowledgeable and sounds intelligent enough for other students to believe. They are here for the purpose of entertaining themselves or, more maliciously, want to entertain themselves by annoying you and others. These students don't often appear on your class roster, but when they do appear, you will have your hands full.

Another form of the distractor student type, which are much more common than the malicious ones, are the ones who may merely want their prior learning validated, and they see the classroom as a pulpit for opinions. Clearly, they haven't been taught that that's only the professor's privilege. All jokes aside, this is likely not malicious even though it may seem that way and can disrupt the class just the same.

Keep in mind that the top students in your class will be as annoyed by the distractor as you are. Use these students as allies and classroom enforcers, if possible. More importantly, it's best to smile, be courteous, and recite the following statement when you encounter this behavior: "This is pulling us way too far off topic. Ask me that question in an email and I'll be happy to respond to it in that way."

Staying on Track, Ranked by Rank

Staying on track is a matter of preference for a professor. Here's a quick rundown by academic rank:

- Assistant professor: Has the entire lecture/class schedule planned out and likes to stay on track. No tangents.
- Associate professor: Enjoys going off track a little. Tangents are the spice of life. Students should expect to do more outside class reading.
- (Full) professor: Doesn't know they are on a tangent and students are too confused or too entertained to get them back on track. Students will be going to office hours.

As a potential higher ed lecturer, it is also important for you to understand yourself. Are you easily distractible? If so, you might be easy prey for a student. Some students just get professors off subject to mess with the syllabus schedule, to entertain themselves and other students, or just to spark a conversation because they are bored with the material. Staying on track isn't always essential on any given day; however, when courses are meant to teach to certain specific standards, staying on track is essential over the course of the semester.

The Laptop Student

The laptop student is the student who pulls out their laptop during class and has it opened the entire class session. Gone are the days of using pen and paper to take notes—many students want to be able to type into a document. Despite good evidence suggesting that handwritten note-taking is much more effective for learning and memory (Mueller and Oppenheimer 2014; Van der Weel and Van der Meer 2024), some students will be adamant that they need to use their laptop. However, there may be others for whom it is a learning "accommodation" per the institution's office of student disability services.

Beyond the need to take notes on a digital device, there is a subset of the laptop students who love to fact check you as an instructor. They will look at class notes, the digital textbook, or do random google searches to confirm or refute what you are discussing in class. They can serve as a healthy check to your presentation of the material, and if you can defend your claims without the aid of outside sources, the rest of the class will earn your respect. However, the fact checker can easily become a classroom distraction.

The more pervasive problem with the laptop student is that there is no good way to know whether they are actually taking notes or fact checking, or rather they are just checking text messages, completing homework for another class, surfing the internet, or playing games while also looking at their mobile phone, which is conveniently hidden behind the screen. They may just be using the laptop as an excuse to shield what they are really doing from your sight. In reality, it is not your job to police student behavior insofar as they are not also distracting you or other students who are seated nearby.

Co-Opting the Laptop Student

There are several strategies that can be implemented to combat the laptop student. The first is an outright ban of devices in the classroom. This is becoming increasingly difficult to do because students are able to request and receive special accommodations due to a learning or emotional divergence. If your syllabus has a ban on devices and you grant an accommodation to use a laptop, the student is now "outed" to the rest of the cohort. It's a tricky situation that has become increasingly common. An alternative approach is to co-opt the use of laptops and integrate it into the class time. Make fact-checking and researching information part of the course, being sure to call on the Type Bs from time to time. You can also use the laptop with students who have the textbook downloaded digitally onto their hard drive. They can be volunteered into reading an important chapter section aloud to the rest of the class.

The Casual Student, Sometimes Known as the Sleeper

We all recognize the casual student as a person not particularly engaged in the here and now of the learning process. Our goal is to transform this person into an engaged learner. Education has become too expensive for casual learning. The casual learner may often be an underachiever for a number of reasons.

The sleeper is a subset of the casual student and usually comes in two types: the student who is sleeping because they are actually tired, and the student who is, in effect, dozing off because they are underperforming. The "why" is important. Get to know your students and their circumstances. Does the sleeper have another job? Has the sleeper had breakfast? Think of the sleeper as untapped potential and tap them on the shoulder. We mean, virtually tap so that you do not risk assault charges. (Seriously.) Purely uninterested potential needs to be turned into recognized and valued potential.

The Engaged Student

We develop and present our classes with this as our ideal student type. Engaged learners often will do all assigned readings and will read them critically. They will be more likely to freely answer questions you raise in class. They love to discuss the material, and their very nature tends to foster a sense of community. They will ask you deeper questions after class ends and will likely show up to office hours at least once during the semester. They tend to understand that course subjects are different and will integrate that difference when trying to understand the material you are presenting. Engaged students are flexible and can manage course workloads effectively. But just like the distractor, we would be fools to think this is the dominant or only student type. Smile and try to make more of these. Find active ways to acknowledge and reward their engagement. Fostering engaged students is the goal for us as teachers.

To foster engaged learning behaviors, we should be trying to make the classroom a place of active learning, even if it is a virtual online classroom such as was used for so many Zoom classes during the recent pandemic. Worksheets, breakout chat rooms, problem-solving panels, and other in-class activities are important tools for engaging the casual learner. Minimize their casual opportunities, which also helps uncover the roots of their troubles.

A Study Skills Epidemic

Many students are highly capable, but due to their innate ability to get by without real work in high school, they have failed to achieve a decent skill set for learning and performing. Thus, their performance in higher education suffers. This is why more universities are including study skills courses as part of the first-year experience—this doesn't work as easily for nontraditionals. The rest of the students coming in believe that they failed to gain adequate knowledge or skills or motivation for performance due not to their fault, but the fault of others in the system. (COVID exacerbated this sentiment.) Virtually all members of the first group consider themselves members of the second group. The contingent faculty member needs to figure out what resources these students need to make the shift to being achievers and connect the students to those resources.

Conclusion

Having a basic understanding of your students as people will help you understand them as learners. We should all be fully aware of the problems in generalizing people on the basis of age, socioeconomic status, and other factors. However, there can be benefits in thinking of how students differentiate among themselves and whether or not there are any patterns we can use that help us more fully address their needs. This can increase our effectiveness in teaching, especially if we are willing to treat any assumptions as working hypotheses, subject to testing and immediate modification. We have made some generalizations largely to get started thinking about students. Most of us tend to think others are like us. If we applied ourselves vigorously as traditional learners, perhaps it is harder for us to think of others who do not apply themselves or who are not "traditional" learners. We all have recollections of how we saw other students around us during our own education. We know stereotyping can be harmful labeling, as in "class clown," which could be kindlier termed "fun learner" if we must label. Perhaps, you may recognize some of the labels and terms used in this chapter as descriptive of things you have seen in your own experience.

We can see a benefit in thinking of the course you teach as part of a continuum of a student's education. That student may be in the middle of a four-year full-time sprint through a bachelor's degree, or a multiyear path of occasional courses as a lifelong learner with no particular degree goals. Knowing how the course you teach fits into the student's overall pattern of life and education will help you tailor aspects of the course to best serve the student's needs and desires. Today's busy, multiple-input life scenarios mean that the student is making sorting decisions earlier, longer, and more frequently than in the past. It is not easy to anticipate how these changes occur going forward, but we can discern some patterns looking back. For example, the wave of returning military veterans after World War II changed the face of education. The grizzled veteran, now a freshman, did not necessarily want to wear the beanie hat of his (or her) predecessors, and often went to night school while working at a full-time job and raising a family. Further, education became more accessible to people from all walks of life. So, educators had to rethink the generalizations and structures of learning modes and classroom delivery models. Today, we continue to see advances in making education accessible to people of all sorts, and to increasing diversity of learners.

One of the consequences of such influence and change is the increased consumerism approach to education. Knowing this improves our effectiveness in responding to it. If the student is purchasing something, what is it? Remind them it isn't the course itself; it is the knowledge and ability to learn that they gain from the course—that is the "product."

We can take a flexible approach to the delivery of our courses and in how we see our students. We can also see academic institutions increasing their flexibility in providing support services for their students. Further, the aging of populations has led to increased student recruitment to keep schools going. Competing *for* students rather than *among* students. Quite a change from the baby boomer era of "if you don't wanna be here go ahead and leave, someone else will take your place." This increasing flexibility and focus on student expectations need not be a bad thing. It can help you grow as an instructor and it can help students become reflective learners, boosting the metacognition for both.

Education is an individual experience for each student, yet we have to teach to a class of many students, not a one-on-one private course. How do we achieve this dualistic balance? The trick as an instructor is how to package and deliver a course that is one course, yet encourages each student to meet individual learning goals within the context of that course. It is at once a group experience and a very personal one.

Embrace the variety of students you find in the classroom. Embrace the variety of backgrounds they have. Diversity represents breadth in approaching and solving problems. The classroom is all about learning to recognize and solve problems—literally and figuratively, so diversity is an asset. The greater reach of admissions recruiters into people from all walks of life means you will get some students for whom college is the fulfillment of a lifelong dream, and others who are just awakening to the possibilities of what college offers—and you get to be a part of that fulfillment and that awakening. Some students find themselves in situations that challenge their abilities and skill sets, so you will have to be aware of resources that can help them. Again, this has changed greatly from the past, when teachers were more likely to just come in, deliver their course without thinking about the context of it to the student's ability to learn. Now there are many college support services, organizations, and departments that can help.

As you might suspect, one of the most rapid changes in education is in technology (yes, yes, we know you can go into many colleges and still find a vintage professor using their overhead transparencies in front of perplexed students). Even if you graduated within the past few years, you may find that online learning systems for course management have changed, becoming more complicated as part of becoming more powerful and "intuitive." So, you will have to do some exploring and learning to see what options you have and what your students typically expect for their course deliveries. Think of this as improving your options for making customizable learning paths for students in your course. You can have multiple strategies. That student who is reluctant to speak out in class may shine in posting online materials and comments. Your use of a hybrid delivery system may make your course that much more accessible to the single parent working as commuter student. Your requirement of in-class presence and participation may be the spark to get the unmotivated entropy-challenged student involved.

CHAPTER 4

Preparing a Course and Running a Class

How Do You Prepare for the Academic Semester?

Ask this question to any professor and you are bound to receive either a troubled look or an unconcerned shrug, and (definitely) differing responses. The regular faculty, especially professors, are blessed and cursed with flexible schedules to work on their scholarly interests, their teaching responsibilities, and their service/committee work from semester to semester. Professors at four-year institutions and especially at research-heavy universities generally make their own schedule and are only confined by when classes start and end. This relatively open nature of time scheduling for those who do not punch a clock can lead to stress, anxiety, and frustration if time is not structured enough.

The adjunct, on the other hand, usually just has to focus on fitting their teaching load with their regular professional work. Granted, that professional work can be just as time consuming or more time consuming than what academics face. However, picking up a course to teach at the local college is a choice. As we discussed earlier, most contingents are motivated by other metrics. But beware: the academy will be waiting for any hint that you can be seduced into providing service as well. Also, professionals who work as adjunct lecturers may be interested in research opportunities with academic partners, but this will be largely outside the boundaries of the contracted teaching position.

As a contingent faculty member, you will have much less flexibility with choosing your academic schedule compared to full-time faculty. Most likely you will be accepting a teaching assignment based on your department's schedule and needs and building your related advising/office hours (read: "student hours") around your assigned class-teaching times. You will also have to fit in classroom and/or laboratory preparation, posting materials, accessing the library, photocopying and related course materials preparation, and course-related research around those times except for what you can do from elsewhere. Fortunately, it is getting easier to do things off campus or remotely, but you still might want to find time to be physically present in the department office or classroom. Ideally, you front-load much of the work so the course can unfold smoothly from the very beginning. Again, all this is in addition to your regular nonacademic job.

Finally, since most institutions boosted their use of them in response to a certain global pandemic, you will have to spend time in advance to learn the course management system software (better known as learning management systems or LMS) and how to utilize university services in the context of course delivery. The more you can plan out in advance, set a schedule, and follow it, the better your chances of successful time management and course delivery.

Asking Questions

As you plan your course, begin with the most basic questions about the context of the course. What level is it? For most, this is immediately discernible from the numbering system as in a 100-level course is for freshmen, 200 for sophomores, 300 for juniors, and 400 for seniors. But it can become more subtle, for example a 500-level course may be for first-year graduates and high-performing seniors. Your assigned course will have a prefix, which indicates perhaps its authoring or originating department or subject area, and it will have a title. What is the title? For example, if it has "seminar" in the title then a certain type of delivery and structure may be presumed. How many credit hours or units is the course? This will reflect the number of hours you are expected to meet, and resultantly, your pay.

Is the course required for a major, a minor, or a concentration? Who is eligible to take it? Can nonmajors or nonmatriculated students take the course? Is it a general education course? How does it fit into the department or program's curriculum? This will inform you about your audience and it will help guide recruitment for the course (upper level and/or elective courses often need to be "sold" to students). You will want to know if anyone else has taught or will teach this course or sections of it. Some courses are designed to address particular issues or specific "deficiencies" that have cropped up in the past and need to be addressed. This may even include things to be unlearned (e.g., common fallacies and false assumptions). The answers to these questions may help you determine what instructor orientation and approach is best for success in teaching this course.

You will want to know who else needs to know about this course. Does the curriculum director, department chair, or others need to approve or receive copies of the syllabus? How does this course offering affect other departments? Perhaps the course engenders or benefits from relationships outside the college. How will this course affect transfer students who may not have had the usual prerequisites at your host site? Will the course benefit from guest lecturers? Is there a pool of these guests from the past offerings?

You may have questions to ask yourself or the department about the course characteristics. Right away you will want an idea of how many students you will have, as this will affect delivery modes, activities, assessments, and course logistics. You may want to know if the course has an accompanying laboratory portion or lecture portion, and if so, are these integrated or separate. You will want to know if you are expected or able to do anything outside of the classroom, such as field trips, library or computer lab usage.

Assumptions about the classroom itself should be kept to a minimum so you don't get too many surprises. If, for example, you really like to use a whiteboard or you want to avoid it because you do not like the off-gassing of the markers, or the dust from chalk in an actual blackboard (yes, these still exist), then arrange to visit the actual or most likely classroom and examine its furnishings. You may find you need to prepare your own kit of markers, erasers, and such, or perhaps your institution is right on the ball with those and it's a nonissue. It is good to know ahead of time.

Other questions deal with the support structure. Do you have coinstructors, graders, teaching assistants (TAs)? Is the course linked to College Writing or some other course? Do they have a peer mentor program that could assist students in your course? Is there a college librarian that provides resources such as a library research guide or library use assistance? Are there other college/university support tools and resources that you anticipate needing or that are available for referral? Is there support to help you develop assessment tools? Will someone come to observe or evaluate your teaching? Knowing the answers to these questions and what resources are available will help you plan your syllabus.

A Preview for First Timers

Every college and university has some form of center for teaching and learning (CTL, more on this a little later) and many of these centers provide tips for teaching and overall course management, offered in the form of workshops, email newsletters, informational web pages, and blog posts. Also, many university educators like to independently write about teaching and/or university life typically through their own newsletters or personal blogs. So, piggybacking on the previous section on asking questions as well as drawing from these types of sources (De Bruin 2013; Harris 2016), we would like to present novice instructors with some very basic guidelines for getting the ball rolling on your new part-time teaching career.

Talk to Your New Colleagues

This is a very common piece of advice that many adjuncts seem to neglect, probably because some professors appear to be inapproachable and because the adjunct tends to be isolated from other faculty, especially if teaching online, evenings, or off-campus. Though this lack of connection is sometimes merited, most professors want their departments to thrive. And all departments want to have as many majors as possible. Students are attracted to departments and programs not only through a strong combination of a passion for the subject but also through notoriety of the professors, either from research productivity or from good word of mouth about their teaching acumen. So, really, reach out and talk to your new colleagues.

Michael Harris, a professor of higher education at Southern Methodist University, explains in a 2016 blog post that many novice instructors often struggle to align their teaching with the established norms of their program, department, and institution. By engaging with colleagues, you can get answers to those questions posed earlier, especially the typical student profile in your assigned course, whether that be student demographics, academic abilities, motivation levels, expectations, and prior knowledge of the subject from early level coursework. This insight will help you tailor your approach to better meet the needs of your students and the expectations of your institution (Harris 2016).

Specify Learning Goals First

This suggestion comes from De Bruin (2013) when she was a graduate student at the Yale Teaching Center and is something we have discussed a lot over the years. Identify at the beginning how you want your students to be different at the end of each lecture and ultimately at the end of the semester. This will not only drive the content you place into the course but also prevent you from gathering materials you won't end up using, thus saving you precious time (for grading, student hours, responding to emails, etc.). If you can limit your lectures to holding two to three learning objectives per one-hour lecture, you will be doing yourself a major benefit down the road. More importantly, readings, class activities, assignments, and exams should all be developed and deployed to serve the goals you establish for your course.

Teach Less Content

This is a tough habit to break but there is no reason to fill class time with nonstop new material. It makes class preparation a nightmare and people can only retain so much new information in a single spell (Russell, Hendricson, and Herbert 1984). You don't need to impress anybody at this point. You already got the teaching gig. Even if you are doing it because you are so passionate about the material you just cannot help yourself, take a pause and scale it back. Students will only remember a few things from each class and in actuality just a few things from each course. They will most likely remember how they felt about your class, so you might as well make an impact with a condensed set of learning items that they can use in the future and a process for learning that they can apply in other classes or at work.

Someone Probably Taught This Already

Another classic piece of advice from virtually all educators: don't reinvent the wheel. Unless you are teaching a class in an entirely new subject area where you are one of the few experts that exist on the planet, you can find an already produced lecture on virtually any subject. Whether that be from your colleagues, from a book publisher who produces supplementary lecture materials as an incentive to use their book, or from the wider internet, use what already exists to manage your limited time. Of course, add your flavor, but this piece of advice will help tremendously with course planning and management.

Use the Teaching and Learning Center

CTLs have been established in over 1,200 colleges and universities across the United States (Wright 2023; Lieberman 2018). At many schools, these centers originated to introduce faculty to new technologies that they could use in instruction. CTLs now serve as hubs for improving teaching practices, rooted in pedagogical theory. Additionally, they are charged with supporting collaboration across departments. They help faculty innovate in teaching to improve student outcomes and align their objectives with institutional missions. Reviewing CTL websites, attending workshops, or reaching out for help undoubtedly falls into the category of "unpaid work," but the payoff for you will be time saved in the long run and a probable contract renewal.

Save Your Work

This is advice that should be used for any work-related task that will be repeated. If you have a positive experience teaching and intend to continue teaching in the future, make sure you stay on top of your organization. Take notes on the effectiveness of your lectures, on activities that took well to the students, and if possible, keep a journal of your classroom time. In short, save all documents that worked and note all that didn't. These will all be extremely useful to you when you teach the class again and will help you create a template for other courses you may teach in the future.

We'll dive a little deeper into some of these suggestions, but if you can do these six things from the start, you will be ready to do well teaching at a college.

Different Approaches to "Prepping" for a Semester of Teaching

An academic semester in the United States typically runs for 15 or 16 weeks in the fall followed by a 4-week break in winter and another 15 or 16 weeks in spring.[*] Students get additional breaks within the semester (especially in spring), but academics are typically busy during those breaks keeping the semester material up to date, including revisiting the course schedule, catching up on grading papers or exams, and various other responsibilities that come with keeping the class on track to completion. Professors do take some time to be around family (they may even interact with them), but are not ignoring their courses when on break, even if the skeptics believe otherwise.

At most academic institutions, there is an expectation that the lecturer will provide some form of instruction on days officially scheduled by the university. Most universities have adopted a two-classes-per-week-per-course schedule, with run times of 75 minutes per class. In lieu of a two-classes-per-week course, you also can find longer

---

[*] About 95 percent of colleges and universities in the United States use the semester system. The rest, notably the California state system, tend to use the quarter system of four 10-week sessions (Marshall 2023).

one-class-per-week lectures that run 2 hours and 30 minutes. These are typically reserved for long discussion format courses. Either way, it is expected that you will be with your students learning in class roughly 150 minutes per week. (Note: Lab courses typically run once a week for two-and-a-half to three hours.)

There are a variety of teaching methods and course matter that dictate the amount of time needed to prepare for class time; however, perhaps the most important variables involved are lecturer experience with teaching and command of the subject matter. Just as every student is a little bit different in how they approach studying and how they organize and budget their time, academics are equally different. There is no apprenticeship for being a university instructor during grad school, so you will find that many academics have discovered their own brand of teaching, for better or for worse. On a completely new course where the instructor needs to work through a syllabus, prepare individual classes that keep pace with the assigned textbook or textbooks, prepare weekly in-class assignments, homework, and eventual exams or term papers, time needed to adequately prepare can quickly add up. This is especially important for academics who feel the need to be in total command of every bit of course material.

Over many years of unofficially polling fellow academics and their course preparation routines, we estimate that it takes anywhere from 30 minutes to 10 hours to prepare for a single lecture. Novice instructors who are still not fully comfortable with teaching and are still gaining familiarity with the subject matter can easily fall into the 10-hour-per-lecture trap. This is an extreme number, but more common than you would expect. In such cases they can expect that on the first attempt, one 16-week course that contains about 25 class meetings could easily take them 250 hours to adequately prepare for the course. That amounts to roughly 10 24-hour days to complete preparation on one course. If the academic is choosing to only put in an eight-hour workday (how dare they!), it would take three times as long or roughly one month to adequately prepare for one course.

Early Career Teaching Investments

Preparing new courses is upfront work that can pay off in the future. If the early career academic is teaching three separate brand-new courses in one semester (not atypical for a tenure-track position), it is reasonable to expect it to take up to three months of time to complete the preparation. Imagine spending your summer, typically off-contract, getting three new courses ready and still having to find time to do your scholarly work or complete any commitments you made to your academic department or university committees you agreed to work on? Nights, weekends, and holidays become fair game in this scenario. As an adjunct, you do not have the luxury of assuming that you are going to teach those new courses you developed on a regular basis, and you need to keep a close eye on potential "return on investment."

Mid-Career Efficiency

For permanent faculty as well as adjuncts, the mid-career academic can easily drop those 10 hours to 3 hours per lecture when preparing for a new course. But the reason for that is they've already put in the upfront investment of time and experience that allows them to be more efficient at creating lecture material. The mid-career academic typically can draw from other previous courses they have taught with similar content. They also are less scared to ask colleagues for their course materials, from which they can adapt content for this new course offering. They also probably utilize the publisher resources that are now widely available for instructors who adopt a certain textbook. It's the "proverbial carrot" that publishers use to convince you to use their book. Lecturers can nimbly integrate preprepared presentation slides, homework, and exams into their 16-week semester, saving a significant amount of time in the preparation. But again, the main reason for this is that they are now benefiting from the compounding effects of time and experience in the craft of teaching. This is particularly effective for introductory courses where textbook sales are much larger than for advanced and specialized texts.[†]

Seasoned Teachers Need Less Time

Now we come to the tenured, full professor who's been teaching for 30 or so years, again with parallels for the experienced adjunct. Full professors are the most expensive employees on a university's ledger, and they often need to be treated with care. But if you can entice them to teach a new course, they probably only need 30 minutes to one hour to prepare per lecture. Chances are they have taught some version of the course in the past, they know the material extremely well, and they have mastered the craft of lecturing and class management. The bold ones will tell you, "Give me two weeks and the textbook, and I'll be good to go." For them, the largest amount of time outside of class likely will end up coming from grading papers and holding office hours. This, again, is indicative of the compounding benefit of time and experience. The full professor is also likely to invite guest lecturers to speak on topics that they are experts in. It may seem like poor form, but it actually helps students learn more effectively when they can listen to a different voice over the course of those 16 weeks.

Shortcuts

We mentioned earlier that shortcuts exist to reduce preparation time such as using a publisher's textbook supplemental material or using a colleague's existing materials, and these are shortcuts that the contingent professor should also adopt. An academic department that is well-organized and dependent on contingent faculty should empower you to use, for lack of a better term, "canned" material, such as an already existing syllabus, lecture notes and slides, quizzes, homework, and exams.

In a part-time capacity, you do not have the luxury to spend a month of your summer preparing for a course for no compensation. In fact, we urge contingents to resist the urge to change much in that first

---

[†] We will resist commenting on how some of our advanced textbook sales royalties have run up into the tens of dollars.

offering, especially if they envision teaching long term. This is especially true for faculty inexperienced with using the LMS. At most institutions, it will be expected to populate the system with weekly content—that is, post lecture notes, homework sets with solutions, topic discussion boards, and so on. American students, especially since COVID, expect all learning materials to be provided online so that they can learn in person or just using the LMS. Some students will even claim it is unfair to use the whiteboard (chalkboard for some of us) in-person without also providing the same material online. If you are orienting (better known as "onboarding") as a new contingent, be sure to get a read from your hiring department on how they handle course delivery in terms of materials, student expectations, and departmental practices. Yes, it is your call, but when you are first getting established you want to be in the same general ballpark as your colleagues.

Your hiring department will be using an adjunct as either a one-time specialty course offering, or to fill in a gap caused by understaffing or other resource-related issues. If the latter, you are far more likely to be looking at a repeat contract offering of the same course, which gives you a greater return on investment for developing your course materials. Also, if the latter, you can look at gradually improving and refining your "toolkit" of course materials, knowing there's a good chance of multiple use of it.

The Syllabus: A Course Design and Management Document

Now to the most important document used in a college class—the syllabus. The syllabus is a contract—both literal and social. It is *the* planning document for course design and management. At its most basic, a syllabus contains essential information the academic institution requires you to present. At its most creative, it is a learning tool and visionary guide for students and yourself. Creating a good syllabus is practically an art form, despite administrative attempts to make it a standardized and mostly legal document.

You will likely be given a course description and some learning goals for the student to achieve through your course. From them you may develop course objectives, action steps to meet those objectives, and assessment tools to see what worked, and if the student "learned." If you are teaching to professional majors, these objectives may be tied to credentialing requirements. You will have to put specific boilerplate language into the syllabus, such as meeting times, advising hours, nondiscrimination policies, where to get assistance, and so forth. In some cases, you might be taking over a course where the syllabus is mostly prepared and you just deliver it. You should be able to determine how much you can add your own "spin" to it. As mentioned in the previous chapter, let it help you set the tone for your class, especially your expectations for the students.

Ironically, the more you put in your syllabus, the less likely students are to read it because it is long. Yet the more that is in it, the more important and useful it becomes in the design of the course. It is a place to sort out and articulate what will happen, how it will happen, why it will happen, how it will be assessed, how the course will "unfold" during the semester, and myriad other things. It also provides you an opportunity to lay down rules and regulations in the likely event of a requested accommodation. It can anticipate and fend off future challenges. Any number of times we have had students challenge our stated requirements that students access the online LMS to find course materials and file assignments and have been able to point them to the paragraph about this in our syllabi.

Easter Eggs in the Syllabus

For those who remember DVDs, it was common practice for movie studios to include "easter eggs" within them. These hidden features included extra footage, gag reels, and sometimes behind the scenes documentaries. Academics co-opted this practice to place a prompt or an assignment for a student to complete upon reading the syllabus. It can be anything from a quote, to a phrase that students must relay to the instructor, or simply just a request to email the professor acknowledging they read the syllabus. These syllabus easter eggs can be placed anywhere within the document. If completed, the student usually earns a few bonus points on a test or equivalent. Though some view this practice as deceptive and in poor form, many others adopted it to prove that most students don't actually read the syllabus. In lieu of this practice, many faculty now just use the first day to read through the entire document so that everyone has reviewed its contents at least once.

Syllabus Nuts and Bolts

If you do a simple web search with keyword phrase "Syllabus Design," you will probably load results from CTLs located at the top-tier schools (they typically get weighted highly in search metrics). We performed one as an exercise for writing this section and got "hits" from Yale, Vanderbilt, Berkeley, Harvard, and MIT. They are all good schools with significant investment going to their CTLs. Their content has a high credibility score among academics, so you probably can trust them.

According to these schools, a syllabus is composed primarily of the following:

- Basic course information
- Instructor information
- Course description
- Learning goals and objectives
- Required materials
- Schedule (including readings and assignments)
- Assessments and grading
- Course policies
- Academic integrity statement
- Diversity statement
- Accessibility statement
- Student academic and wellness support resources
- "Subject to change" disclaimer

We encourage you to use top college CTLs to help with syllabus development, especially with respect to anything specific within these highlighted elements, but definitely rely on your institution's and your department's resources, requirements, and recommendations for the foundation of your work. Additionally, here are some words of wisdom on some of the elements you will likely have to think about as you complete this important document.

Goals and Objectives

Again, the best way to design your class is to think about what you want students to be able to do. In the syllabus, describe this in concrete, tangible, and assessable ways and in the context of addressing "deep questions" (Bain 2004) or "capacious questions" that begin with goals and conclude with action steps, activities, and products (SENCER 2023). Overarching goals are concrete and measurable. We should be able to tell when we've met them. Rather than just teaching a particular topic, think of the course as enabling students to solve problems. What kinds of problems do we want them to be able to tackle? What will they be able to do as a result of the course?

Some goals involve lower order thinking skills such as knowledge, comprehension, and application (Bloom's Taxonomy of Education Objectives, in McGuire and McGuire 2015), which might be expressed with words such as listing, recognizing, reciting, paraphrasing, explaining, and calculating. Other goals involve higher order thinking skills such as analysis, synthesis, evaluation, and some aspects of application that might be expressed with words such as derive, design, formulate, interpret, analyze, and predict.

Verbs such as interpret, construct, formulate, solve, analyze, and predict are indicative of goals that extend beyond simply recalling, reciting, or explaining what was covered in class. Such terms reflect an ability to operate with the basic knowledge presented in the course. Accordingly, instead of having a goal to "recognize and describe a biogeochemical cycle," we might say "be able to interpret environmental conditions based upon reports of carbon loading and storage."

Sample goals focus on higher order thinking skills. Make it action based. Say "At the end of this course, I want students to be able to _____." Basic skills such as being able to identify plants using a dichotomous key are embedded in higher order goals. Ancillary skills are skills that may be related to the course but are not primary. Ancillary skills might include being able to work in groups, being able to write a laboratory report, be able to apply basic statistics, be able to properly cite references, be able to make a PowerPoint presentation and deliver it. You do not want to have too many of them—it bogs down your course, so just pick some essential ones that provide context for the course in relation to the majors it supports, and perhaps the "general education" curriculum.

Ideally, a course will have an overall goal and no more than a few objectives in support of that goal. These should be articulated in a clear manner. A good objective is something measurable and achievable. Active verbs are helpful. Be direct and concrete. For example, "Be able to write a Phase I Environmental Site Assessment report" is a specific task and achievement, whereas "Understand the process of site assessment" is vague and hard to measure. The objectives should support the overall course goal, which is likely created from the assigned catalog course description. As an adjunct, you might be given the course goal and objectives. If this is not the case, then you should develop them. If the goal and objectives are vague and difficult to measure, check with your chairperson or whoever has the lead on the course sections, and see if they agree to refine them or will let you do so.

Scheduling

Preparing for the academic year is all about planning. You must design how the course will "unfold" as the semester progresses. You will need the lead time to make room and equipment reservations, schedule invited speakers, field trips, and events. Be prepared to find that the college holidays and days off might be different from what the public observes. To make this even more confusing, some colleges have staff holidays but still hold classes. You also must keep in mind when various religious holidays or other commitments occur. The registrar will have a calendar available so you can tell on what days no classes are being held. Just do a basic web search with keyword phrase "[Your School] Academic Calendar" and you will likely find your school's academic calendar.

Attendance

Know your attendance policy ahead of time so you can put it in the syllabus. Usually, such policy is at the discretion of the individual faculty member but course accreditation and academic institution accreditation mandates a certain number of contact hours (though not easily enforced). The department may have a cancellation policy they want you to use. Keep in mind the nature of your students and where the course is located. For example, students who live on campus do not have to worry about the car breaking down on their commute. Students in certain parts of the country have to be aware of winter storms, tornadoes, and the like. You don't want anyone to risk their life to attend your class. At commuter schools and many others, this question may be decided for you via public announcements and text or email notifications. Since it is not high school, you do not necessarily have to have the student provide a note from their doctor if they are sick; you are entitled to take their word for it. You are also entitled to advance notice when possible and to expect the student to make up the missed work on their own.

Canceling a Class

What do you do if you have your own conflicts? If you have your own work schedule that interferes with a class meeting, you can schedule the students to work independently or online or get a soon-to-be-former friend to cover your class. (This assumes that you do not have a TA assigned to your course, which is a good assumption.) A certain number of contact hours are expected/required for accredited courses, so be leery of simply canceling a course meeting. Yes, students complain when they get their money's worth, but even more when they don't get it. They will unhappily let others know when a class is canceled at the last minute, especially if the only reason they are on campus that day (or got up early or stayed up late) is to attend your class. Better to plan ahead in the syllabus and course outline for any deviations from regular class meetings. Your academic department chair should be able to advise you, as should the department administrative assistant—often the most knowledgeable person about such things on the campus. It is good for the department chair to not find out that class was canceled by seeing a note on the door or hearing after the fact from a student, which will definitely happen.

Safety and Emergency Preparedness

In the post-COVID era, you might have better access to recorded lecture resources either from things you may have created (or will create) or from video resources found on the internet. Be mindful that in inclement weather, some students may not be able to access the internet due to localized outages. Some other students will take advantage of this potential issue and not do the remote work assigned. It's something that you'll have to navigate, but only worry about it if it becomes a habit for a particular student. Use the "fool me once shame on you fool me twice shame on me" adage to get you through those circumstances.

Flexible Delivery Options

Some professors that have been teaching the same course or courses over many years will brag that they offer courses in a "Hyflex" format (see Columbia 2020), where they offer live lectures and identical lectures online so that students may choose which format to use, at their convenience. Hyflex or not, this is beyond what most faculty are expected to do and only realistic to offer using a great deal of resources and time. However, this became an unofficial expectation during and after the days of teaching during the pandemic (AKA the great teaching pivot). Do not feel bad if you cannot accomplish

> this feat on an adjunct's time and budget. If you want to offer this, negotiate extra money in the contract to do it.

Discussions

Online and in-person discussions can be uncomfortable for some students. There may be a perfectly valid reason to use discussions anyway and if you have already put into the syllabus your plan for use of discussions and why you are using them, it will seem much less arbitrary for students. Ease discomfort by providing some ground rules, and if possible, for alternatives. (Note some students with diagnosed social anxiety may have "Letters of Accommodation" for your institution that can inform use of alternatives. You may also find the need to refer a student who does not yet have a Letter of Accommodation.)

For online discussions, you can promulgate a "netiquette" (rules for behaving online) from one of many examples available from your institutional CTL and various other sources. Students benefit from classroom and online rules of civility. They also benefit from guided structure, such as asking them to pose a question to the group and provide their opinion of a suitable answer from their perspective. There are ways to tailor discussions in a way that reinforces quiet students to participate.

Assessments

There are various forms of assessment used in college classes. Course content can often dictate the types of assessments you will use in your course, especially if teaching to preprofessionals or artists. Core classes for the university curriculum or for a program major tend to skew more toward exams and papers, while discussions and portfolios tend to be used in upper level and art classes. We touch on some finer points of the most basic assessments in the following.

Exams

Exams are not just for summative assessments. Research has established that the very act of taking a test helps students retain class materials superior to students who are not tested (Gooblar 2019). There are many different formats for tests. These formats affect the way your time is distributed. For example, good multiple choice questions that test critical thinking rather than simple recall or educated guessing are practically an artform to produce. They take a great deal of upfront work, but you can develop a bank of them for rotational use. And you can grade them fast. "Write an essay" questions are easy to create but take more work in grading. We are all familiar with other formats such as short answer, matching, true or false, and the like. A quiz usually uses one format, maybe two. An exam may be a variety and take up the entire class time.

Test taking is a skill, which means it can be learned and improved upon. Also make sure to help your students know how to take exams. Even something as simple as dressing up for an exam can improve test scores (Fang 2023). It seems obvious, but students forget effective strategies such as using effective learning strategies, rewriting notes, making practice exam questions, setting study times and partners. (See McGuire and McGuire 2015, 117–118 for a good summary of test-taking strategies and advice.) Remind students to visit their campus learning center and to look at their institution's postings for test preparation and stress management. Some courses and departments provide peer tutors and TAs that prepare students for improved exam performances. Students may not realize that some instructors are only waiting to be asked to lead or provide review sessions. Myers (2023) suggests using the free online site Quizlet for making virtual flashcards for practice. There are many excellent online sources for study techniques and tools.

Immediate Feedback After an Exam Helps

Students will tolerate slow return on homework and other similar assignments, but often expect you to return exam scores as soon as possible, if not sooner. Trying to give at least some feedback immediately helps so the test results get resolved quickly. Giving students the opportunity to research and explain the answers to questions they missed on an exam can be an alternative; they can receive partial credit of some form for making the corrections to wrong answers. This alleviates some of the stress and it also improves student learning in areas where their performance needs improvement. It may help you to know that the literature shows that even students who do poorly on tests benefit from them because tests can improve their learning (Carey 2014). Nevertheless, some seasoned instructors provide alternatives to tests, specifying in advance via the syllabus that students can do either a test or some other form of assessment that demonstrates equivalent learning.

Quizzes

A quiz counts for less points than an exam or test, and a quiz is usually shorter. Otherwise, they are the same. A frequent problem with the use of testing is its perception as a source of stress to students. Yet large class size and other factors may mean you have to use exams and quizzes. Or perhaps you are preparing students for a career in which tests are necessary for professional licensing and certification. Tests and quizzes are often just a fact of life and students should have some preparation to deal with them. Fortunately, there are some things you can do to lessen stress in addition to making sure your use of testing is judicious. Practice and preparation help. You can lower the weight assigned to the test. You can shorten it, so it becomes more quizlike. You can allow students to take practice tests or practice questions that might appear on tests. Quizzes are especially useful for a student's first encounter with you as an instructor as they will be wondering what to expect from you.

Term Papers

There are some dangers in using these, particularly in these days of growing use of AI, and an already established market of available term papers for purchase or sharing. Book-report-type papers can be done that avoid deep critical thinking. The use of staging in report development and review can help with some of these issues. By staging, we refer to the formative assessment strategy of development of progressive tools in the report that the student submits, gets feedback on, and builds upon so their formal report is informed and improved. Students appreciate the control this gives them in being able to predict how the final report will be perceived (i.e., "graded") by you. Some common stages include selection of topic/subject area, "thesis statement," notes, annotated bibliography, outline, first drafts. Final draft, proofed, and corrected final version. This is also a good opportunity to incorporate peer reviews, which you can remind students is a normal procedure in the work world.

Term papers for advanced courses in refined or obscure subject areas are less subject to plagiarism because they are more specialized, as in the use of "technical reports," but like any writing, it is subject to exploitative use of AI. You can preempt this to a certain degree by actually suggesting that students use AI to help develop outlines or early drafts. You can then advise the students of some of the dangers of AI usage (especially improper use, lack of references, improper emphasis or ranking). You will find the college librarians are only too happy to be invited to the class to discuss searching and crediting of information. Software such as SafeAssign and Turnitin can detect plagiarism. Your institution will likely have specific detection software that you can use to catch the more flagrant instances of plagiarism. Hopefully, you already have in your syllabus a statement of expectation that students will do their own work. You can decide how much to deal with plagiarism in your syllabus, informed by advice from your department chair and the institution's policies.

Short Papers or "Mini Papers"

An advantage of short papers of one to two pages is that they are "low stakes" in terms of your design work, student effort, and grading. You can use them to see if the student has done the reading or you can go beyond that to encourage critical thinking. The student may not realize that it is actually harder to write a short paper than one several pages longer because it requires greater efficiency. This exercise promotes student skills in summarizing and synthesis. It is also a bit harder to find a short essay among the online term paper mills and vendors and a two-page AI-written mini paper is almost always easy to sniff out.

Portfolios

Portfolios give students an opportunity to select their best examples of work products and course achievements and represent a common "real life" work practice. Some programs, notably art schools, require students to regularly assemble and maintain portfolios. Many of us consultants in the outside world have portfolios of our projects that we can show clients. Getting our students in the habit of thinking along these lines is a good practice for them. It tends to help them produce better products because they start to think of them as something for outside consumption, not just something seen by a teacher briefly for grading.

Portfolios are sometimes used as qualifiers to enter a course or program, as in submitting an art portfolio to be accepted into an MFA program. Or they are used as a final, summative assessment, as in submitting a portfolio of work upon completion of a course or program of study. But they can be effectively used as an ongoing formative tool that both documents a student's progress and the student's cognition about that progress.

A common danger of portfolios, aside from students not knowing how to assemble one, is the tendency to give them last minute attention. Using progress checks can help students develop their portfolios as the semester unfolds. To prepare students for peer reviews and your reviews have them comment on the items they choose for their portfolio. Your feedback in conjunction with their own and that of others can help steer them toward a positive final assessment. The portfolio can be a significant grade item or you can use it as an option in place of an exam or other assignment.

Textbooks

Textbooks remain a thriving industry, despite the prevalence of online content. In an introductory course like Calculus or Biology, adjuncts will be assigned a textbook. If teaching for the first time, it is not worth asking to use a different text. If you find a better explanation in another book, just provide it to the students as a supplement. Some mid-career instructors become adamant about using a specific text; however, unless it is tied to a very specific subject offered as an upper course elective, it really isn't worth the time.

You will commonly find that textbooks are offered in print, as an etextbook, bundled with print and etextbook versions, and sometimes refashioned into a phone or tablet app. As mentioned earlier, most textbook publishers will provide an accompanying webpage or a full website for a textbook, which may include student and instructor resources. These often contain answers to end-of-chapter questions (students usually can access the odd-numbered question answers while instructors with proper credentials can access all numbered question answers and sometimes fully-worked-out solutions). They routinely include Microsoft PowerPoint slides for each chapter. Some publishers also provide preformatted question pools that can be integrated into the LMS.

Using textbooks as a means to organize your syllabus (and by extension the semester schedule) is a logical and time-saving practice. Again, do not reinvent the wheel. Select the chapters that fit most closely to your course goals and objectives and use those to structure your semester-long agenda. Having a textbook as the backbone of your course also allows you to "go off script" in the classroom. Some students might complain that in-class material is disconnected from the textbook reading and the overall schedule, but having the flexibility to address unexpected (but welcomed) discourse in the classroom on the condition that students "catch up" by reading that week's textbook chapter content is an acceptable trade-off for most of the class.

Is It Unethical to Require Your Own Textbook?

The short answer to this question is: No. But students might think so unless it gets explained to them that you wrote the textbook because you could not find anything better to do the job, and that if they were to calculate the compensation you received for this three-year project with the $127.03 annual royalty check, it adds up to a negative amount once you deduct your expenses. We regularly calculated the few dollars compensation we would receive from a class's use of our authored textbooks, doubled it, and donated that amount to one of the state's natural resources nonprofits, and put a statement to that effect in the syllabus. However, if you have assembled a package of your own course materials for use by students and want them to purchase it, first be sure you have investigated the institution's resources for assembling and providing these materials as the most cost-effective means. Also note that some institutions will prohibit faculty from charging students for using their book. In that case, you will likely have to provide a free electronic copy that they can access through the LMS.

Course Budgets

Your academic institution should have some kind of economic support for courses beyond merely paying you to teach them. As an adjunct, you are likely the last person to have such fees as a resource. But it is worth checking as part of your course preparations and maybe even as early as during your "onboarding" process. If you are teaching a laboratory course, there is a fair possibility the students have paid some kind of additional fee to contribute toward supplies. But the vast majority of faculty have to assume no particular course budget; so, you will have to keep that in mind in preparing your activities to meet course objectives.

As a working professional you may have access via your "regular" job to potential guest speakers, field trips, equipment demos and the like.

If it is a lab course or a course in a specialty program such as a learning community or honors curriculum, there may even be some kind of course assistance that can help you prepare or provide resources. If you do not have anything available as resources, you may find this stimulates seeking low-cost creative solutions. Online teacher forums, education conferences, and local networks, especially high school ones, excel at providing low-budget activities you can tap into.

Zero-Budget Science Lab

If your course does not have an assigned course fee, you should check with the academic department to see if there are any funds you can access. If not, you may be forced to be creative. We once taught an introductory science course with no laboratory space and no course budget despite objectives to teach scientific method and critical thinking. We introduced a lab activity on dousing that only required a forked stick. Living in a woodland ecosystem we were able to procure forked sticks for the lab at our own "expense" with a quick trip outside. Students found and critiqued articles pro- and antidowsing and designed experiments to test their hypotheses. The low-tech approach reduced student apprehensions and motivated them to experiment. All students were taking the course as their only science course to meet their two-year degree requirements. There is often something you can do to meet objectives if you are creative and don't mind scrounging even if you have no budget. Often you can get tips from K-12 teachers, especially for your introductory courses. You definitely can find items that the department has been squirreling away just waiting for somebody to use again, or for the first time.

Embracing Technology

Address your use of technology and your expectations for students in your syllabus. You might as well admit it, technology needs to be your friend and partner in teaching your course. Your institution will likely use some kind of LMS (described later), so you will have to at least be aware of it. Most institutions require some minimal usage, such as posting of syllabi. But you will likely find that your students expect additional use of it for grades and for posting assigned readings and course materials. Other students might be less familiar with it and need some coaxing to become competent with it. Fortunately, this need not be your job on top of everything else you have to do—point out the many resources available to help students. Hopefully you have laid the groundwork for this in your syllabus, and your preparation has included reserving the necessary technical resources.

Your course will also need to be "digitally compliant." This means your online aspects and use of technology must be inclusive and accessible to all students, including those with disabilities. Plan for this in advance, and with information on the accommodations needed by students who will be taking your course. Your institution should have resources to enable you to achieve this.

Your syllabus should prepare your students for how you expect to teach the course, because that affects how you expect them to learn the material. And it enables them to plan ahead. It also lets you articulate the need for any support structures you need for your methods. These can be anything from clickers for classroom voting to peer TAs for active learning.

Classroom Management

Our concern with classroom management in the planning phase mostly has to do with the general tone of how you plan to teach and interact with your students. You will use this in conjunction with the characteristics of your student demographics to prepare your syllabus. However, each class will have its own "personality." Your classroom management tools can provide ways to deliver the course and achieve student learning in effective ways. Being able to assume a diverse set of behaviors and skills that covers the range of students in your class will help with this. Set some expectations for classroom behavior, and online behavior at the outset in your syllabus and in your introductory narrative on the first day of class. Explain the reason why you are laying out these expectations, and how the student will benefit, then give them your expectations.

Similarly, your classroom management starts with physical space. You should have some choice over this and how students are arranged within it. Do you prefer them sitting in a circle or lined up in rows, or arranged around activity tables? If you must teach a large class, is there room for seat choice? Students will tend to come to the same seat throughout the semester. If you have a large class, can you arrange where students sit so that you can flow among them, or do you prefer to be at a podium in the front? Will you have TAs or peer learning with small groups?

There are ample resources for dealing with the various aspects of classroom management in the literature, online, and in later chapters of this book (in the context of teaching and learning tips); however, we leave here some important aspects to consider that Chilelli (2024) synthesized for TAs at Ohio University:

- Build rapport early on by greeting students, learning their names, getting them to interact with each other, and inviting them to visit your office during student hours.
- Have well-designed and engaging lessons that always highlight the objectives for learning that day, with planned teaching and learning activities, and strategies to check for understanding.
- Have a contingency plan for unexpected events or glitches in technology.
- Build on knowledge through scaffolding: (1) The teacher models the new task or concept; (2) the class (teacher and student) does the task together; 3) the students partner to complete the task in cooperating groups; and (4) students work independently to demonstrate mastery.
- Get your rules straight, make them clear and inclusive, and be consistent.

- Do not take student misbehaviors personally. Remember, the sleeping student may just be tired from pulling an all-nighter.
- Try not to use the same teaching mode throughout the semester. A semester-long PowerPoint show can be too much even for the most motivated students.
- Don't be late to class. Some faculty believe that showing up late adds to their mystique; however, modeling tardiness will usually create insubordination of other rules.

Learning Management Systems

While paper is still used in the classroom, much of the content delivery, management, and assessment are increasingly completed digitally using LMS (sometimes also referred to as course management systems). You may have heard of some of them depending on when you attended college yourself. Examples of LMS systems we have used as professors include Canvas, Moodle, Blackboard, and Brightspace. (Probably some other ones that we are forgetting about.) It is not uncommon for universities and colleges to switch to different software once a licensing agreement expires, so it is best to keep a generic understanding of these systems. You will be offered opportunities to receive some training; however, it is equally likely you will be learning how to use them on the job.

In 2007, William and Sunnie Lee Watson described a generic LMS as a software platform designed to accomplish the following:

1. Design, deliver, and manage instructional content;
2. Identify and assess learning or training goals for an organization;
3. Track the progress toward meeting those goals;
4. Collect and present data for supervising the learning process of an organization as a whole.

According to Watson and Watson (2007), when originally introduced to universities, the LMS was almost exclusively used for online and blended learning courses. They were used primarily to place course materials at a dedicated online location for students to access, to assign enrolled students into specific courses, to store student assignment submissions, to track student performance, and to host and mediate communication between the students (peer to peer) and between student and instructor. Since about 2015 and increasingly since the pandemic began, universities have either mandated or heavily incentivized the use of LMS software for course delivery and grade tracking. From an administrative point of view, the reason for their widespread adoption makes a lot of sense.

First, they are very useful for managing every aspect of a course: you can create and organize courses, modules, and lessons in a manner that follows your syllabus schedule. You can schedule when a weekly module turns on and off, and you can set timers on assignments so that deadlines are hard. Here you can upload documents, video, presentation files, and the like, which allows for better organization and serves as a great record of what you do during the semester in case you teach the course in the future. Also, if something interesting gets discussed in class, you have the option to add content to the weekly module in "real time."

Second, it is very helpful with respect to user management. Since every student has their own email address and university ID number, you can add or drop students from the course relatively easily, which also serves to keep nonmatriculated students from accessing sensitive or protected content (copyright or other consideration). You can also add faculty observers or TAs and assign them different permissions and responsibilities.

Third, grading and assessment features are very helpful to keep students aware of their current effort in your class. LMS software has tools for creating and managing assignments, quizzes, and exams, which are essential when you are delivering an online-only course. For in-person courses where quizzes and exams are not conducive to online delivery, the LMS software gradebook feature is still very useful. Students tend to lose papers now more than ever, so keeping their assignment and test scores in a permanent web-based location is helpful, especially when a student inevitably contests an exam score.

If you are interested in learning more about how faculty use LMS software, you can review a survey conducted by Vanderbilt University, reported by Coble (2016) of the Vanderbilt Center for Teaching.

Some Drawbacks

Despite the many benefits of using LMS software for course management, there are some drawbacks. Most certainly, these are tied to how well you understand how to properly use the LMS software. For example, LMS software often touts the ability to track the amount of time a student spends on a module or assignment. We have experienced this feature to be unreliable.

Also, the grading feature is not always robust. It is good at tracking points, but if you have a formula that weighs assignments differently or if you allow lowest score assignments to be dropped, you have to either learn how the LMS can do that or get frustrated and do that sort of calculation offline. Perhaps the most significant drawback is the amount of time it takes to populate a course with your content and setting up calendar and scheduling features. If you are a supremely organized person, this can take a significant amount of time and sometimes you enter a date or time incorrectly and no students alert you about that until an hour before the deadline. This inevitably creates more work. That said, LMS software is a part of university culture, so you are going to have to get used to using it, even if it is to satisfy a minimal requirement.

Conclusion

Preparing and running a course is a skill, which means it can be learned by most people. There is no secret formula, you mostly just need to be prepared. Consider your syllabus to be the major planning document. Your strategy should be to engage students in concrete ways that minimize their stress. You do this for them by providing predictability. This doesn't mean you cannot shake them up with something like "well, how about for a change let's go outside today." What it does mean is predictability by giving them some control over their performance and how it will be graded.

This starts with setting a tangible overall course goal and supporting objectives that are clearly defined and measurable. It means sharing these with the students, so they know the expectations. They should know what the action steps are that support the objectives; things like assignment descriptions and details, grading rubrics, delivery logistics, and "what ifs."

Your preparation should include contingencies, like what to do if a class must be canceled, or if a guest speaker doesn't show up, or if all the students do miserably on the quiz. Some of this you address in your syllabus, others you address in your course planning. You may decide to have a range of ways in which you can deliver concepts, such as PowerPoints, field trips, class guests, class activities, guided student explorations, or perhaps a combination of these. This gives you flexibility that you can prepare for and that provides intentional stability and structure for your students. Good planning improves creativity because it reduces external stresses and lets you and your students focus on the variation that can meet your course goal and objectives.

Good planning means knowing the technological and institutional supports and constraints. It means knowing what to do if you encounter problems ranging from failing display terminals to disruptive factors, to students in need of support services. It means advocating for the best learning spaces and services for your course on behalf of the students. You cannot anticipate everything, so being able to take things in stride is important. Having flexibility in planning and delivering your course means you can make it "student centered" without needing to compromise your objectives, which are in fact on behalf of the student anyway.

Finally, although a good syllabus will help you get 80 percent of the way to designing a college-ready course, there are still small details that you will want to fine-tune. Rely on your institution's CTL and the various other CTLs out there to help with your course design. The internet allows you to find excellent resources on course design that these programs provide for free (e.g., Washington University in St. Louis 2024). Take advantage of that as you prepare, review, and modify your course materials in preparation for a new course or the next semester.

CHAPTER 5

Teaching Tips

Efficient and Effective Tips

There are teaching tips peppered throughout our chapters on course management, planning, and other matters. Additionally, we highly recommend reading *What the Best College Teachers do* by Ken Bain (2004). At 207 pages, including references, it is an efficient book to read, and often cited by others. Bain reminds us that teaching is not based on the old "transmission model" but rather on the "learning model." Bain reports his research on how the best professors prepare to teach, what they expect of students, how they conduct class, how they treat students, and how they evaluate student learning. Essentially, effective teaching involves creating conditions in which students realize their potential to learn, and that this takes conscientious effort. Gooblar's *The Missing Course: Everything They Never Taught You About College Teaching* (2019) is another text full of excellent advice on promoting effective learning. While you are at it, put Benedict Carey's *How We Learn* (2014) in your list. It will tell you some surprising things about learning.

Even with these recommendations, we think it is helpful to have a dedicated chapter on essential teaching strategies. While reading through this, we advise you to keep in mind that more than anything, the best teachers are effective and efficient and have a knack for playing to their strengths. Do what you are good at and be willing to work on the things you want to improve on. Think back to what you remember as being particularly effective. You can learn a great deal from colleagues. K-12 teachers are especially good informants. There are many tried and true techniques and tools "in the commons" that you can use beyond what we will discuss.

Being Effective and Efficient

We have used the words "effective" and "efficient" several times in the first two paragraphs of this chapter. As adjunct faculty, we have limited time to accomplish a focused mission—achieving our course goals to advance student learning while keeping our students engaged with the subject matter. We work toward doing this by being effective and efficient. For top advice in this area, we particularly like *The Effective, Efficient Professor* by Phillip Wankat (2002)—just look at that title! Start by recognizing the clear distinction between being efficient and being effective, as one does not necessarily follow from the other. Think of efficiency as what you do in teaching and effective as something measured by student learning. There are ways to make teaching effective and efficient and ways to convey teaching. But learning is inherently neither effective nor efficient. Professors need to have faith that the students will learn and have to adapt if (or when) the students are not learning. This likely means you, if you are that professor, will have to change the way you are currently teaching.

You can support adopting new teaching strategies by beginning with the resources readily at hand. As discussed in Chapter 4, CTLs are great resources to help you balance your teaching approach in a way that promotes learning. We draw from several of them with what follows below.

Active Learning

A very common stereotype in college teaching is that a professor stands in front of the classroom and scribbles on a whiteboard while students frantically decipher and copy what is being said and written. Or perhaps more recently, a professor will create a PowerPoint (or equivalent) slide deck and fly through a presentation for an hour with little break in between. This is referred to as passive teaching or teaching for passive learning. This is really a teacher-centered strategy. Yes, this does happen, and professors are "guilty" of doing this from time to time. It is also a hallmark of novice teaching, because the lecture is the most controllable approach to teaching. It is efficient for preparation and delivery in that you prepare, and you present while the students listen and take notes. There is nothing inherently wrong with this method. Students will learn. However, depending on the subject matter, it is not particularly effective. There are other methods that can produce better results, if done correctly.

An alternative teaching approach that is recommended from kindergarten to graduate school is called active teaching, or teaching for active learning. Active learning is an instructional model that engages students in activities that require them to do things: think critically by solving a problem in class, collaborate with peers on answering a question or breaking down a concept, or reflect on a passage using prior knowledge and newly learned insights. This is termed "active" because students are not passively receiving information as they presumably would during a lecture. If you can implement active strategies, studies suggest that students will retain information better, they will improve their problem-solving skills, and ultimately will demonstrate a deeper understanding of course material.

Five Active Learning Techniques

Active learning is commonly defined as "activities that students do to construct knowledge and understanding" (Brame 2016). Techniques to achieve active learning abound and in fact there is an admitted blurriness to what constitutes active learning under such a broad definition. Also, the techniques can be separated into those that supplement traditional lecture learning and those that substitute the lecture altogether. Following are some techniques that you can use during your teaching, inspired by suggestions made by various university CTLs and from our own experiences.

1. **Intermittent Pausing**

    These are two variations of the same technique that you can use, especially when still going heavy on lecture as your primary delivery mechanism. Both involve pausing for 2 to 3 minutes after a 15-minute lecture sequence. The first version recommends making students pair up to discuss and rework their notes. Doing this helps them check their immediate understanding of the material and causes them to check the organization of the lecture. They might reorganize to a structure that they prefer for memorization and comprehension. The second version involves a concept known as retrieval practice. After 15 minutes of lecture material, the instructor pauses and has students write down everything they can remember about what they were being lectured on. Both techniques are effective for promoting deeper learning and rooted in sound theory. You can also use "minute papers" or "think-pair-share" as other techniques related to intermittent pausing (Brame 2016).

2. **Demonstration Reverse Q&A**

Keyword search "Walter Lewin Physics" on YouTube and you will find the most wonderful collection of undergraduate physics class demonstrations. Demonstrations are an excellent supplement to a classroom lecture. However, they often fall into the passive information category because students are not necessarily doing anything during a demonstration. You can remedy this in a number of ways. Recruiting a volunteer always helps. Additionally, you can ask students to make a prediction based on their intuition or based on recently presented material. Once they lock in their answer, maybe discussing with a peer, you then carry out the demonstration to uncover the result. By doing this you reverse the question-and-answer process so that the student has to think critically about the material, formulate an answer to the question, then use the results of the demonstration to reinforce the critical thinking process.

3. **Interactive Quizzes and Polls (AKA Clicker Questions)**

This technique has gained popularity in large auditorium classes that have been updated to accommodate technology. This also involves pausing within a lecture, but this time you display a concept or calculation problem with multiple choice responses. Students have handheld devices that allow them to select answers, which are recorded automatically by the classroom system. This allows the audience to see a polling of all responses in real time and compare their responses to the class as a whole. This can be modified by allowing for before-and-after polling, where students input a response and are then allowed to discuss their response with a classmate, possibly changing the response upon discussion. In small classrooms or environments where technology does not exist, you can substitute clickers with small whiteboards, where students respond, and polling is done by hand.

4. Concept Maps

Concept maps are popular especially in subjects that push students to think about connections in systems. Concepts or ideas are typically placed into boxes and or circles with arrows used to connect related ideas. The concept map has roots in science learning but has been applied to engineering, business, government, and more. Concept mapping activities are very helpful when you want to abandon the lecture paradigm for a day or two. Concept maps test learning, so it is expected that students will have read from the textbook or reviewed an online lecture before attending the class session.

5. Muddiest point

This strategy is a great alternative to lecturing when you need to switch up modalities because you sense that the topic is confusing your audience. In this activity, you ask students to write down the most confusing concept they encountered in a previous lesson or lecture. Collect the responses and review them for the following class. Spend that class day responding to and clarifying these muddy points that the class has. Usually, confusing concepts tend to be confusing across the board and are similar from semester to semester. This is a great way to "unstick" people and to show them that you care about their progress in the class.

The Flipped Learning Trend

When you are an adjunct, you have to be very efficient with your time. When you are in the classroom you want to focus on improving the students' learning. This means the student has to do something outside of the classroom to be ready. So, you will likely hear about "flipping the classroom." In *Teaching Naked* (Bowen 2012; a definite attention-grabbing title), José Bowen discusses flipping the classroom, a recent trend in which the students do work outside of class and come to class ready to engage in applying the results of that exterior work.

We used to call this "coming to class having done your homework." But now it means even more; by "flipping" the classroom, technology can greatly assist learning yet (theoretically) not impede classroom interactions. This requires significant preparation ahead of time and in administration of the course. Dr. Bowen is a wonderful person (we've met him), an engaging speaker, and a heck of a musician, but we could not help noticing that he only teaches one course per semester or less, and when doing so has a number of teaching assistants to help out. As an adjunct, that will not be you.

If you have not figured it out yet, in flipping, the lecture happens online before the in-person class. This can be accomplished because that lecture has been recorded or prepared digitally and made available online. The actual class time is devoted to meaningful discussions, interactions, and activities. Students are expected to review the online lecture prior to attending class so that they can actually contribute to the in-class experience. Flipping can be hit or miss; it depends on student interest levels and how well the teacher is able to present the content before they arrive in class.

Flipping has proved popular in chemistry, physics, mathematics, music, and other subjects. However, to flip a class takes a lot of work, plan for at least three times the work as a normal class by the time you are done converting everything to digital, making the videos, planning assessments, and so forth. This is a real issue for the part-time, contingent professor who wants to "flip" a class. There are also issues from a student perspective. What if the student cannot review everything before the class starts? Many things can interfere—work, family, other classes, pandemics, unforeseen complications.

Also, flipped classes can be problematic in upper level, difficult courses. These tend to be complicated classes in which many students don't come to class having already learned/reviewed the material. The students (and us) rely on the class times to learn the material and then reinforce it after class. Flipped classes can also be problematic in introductory courses, as the students' motivations may not yet be developed, and the content area may be too new for the students to be ready for independent work ahead of time.

Do a keyword search using "flipped classroom" and you will find a plethora of articles about its use in higher education. Indeed, when flipped learning came out as a teaching strategy, it was written about extensively and greeted with polarizing opinions and very little data showing that it is more effective than a traditional model. Now that some time has passed, it is safe to say that flipping learning out of the classroom does not cause harm, so using it is more a preference over being a guaranteed benefit (Yong, Levy, and Lape 2015).

Our opinion is that flipped learning can be good for the basics where students learn at different paces (and bring in different background knowledge) because it allows students to learn at their own pace and learn what they need to learn based on what they already know. Partial flipping is okay but full flipping is probably not realistic for contingents and adjuncts since it is time-consuming and potentially bad for reviews. If you are skilled in this area and think you will be teaching the course multiple times (or at multiple places), then it might be for you. The essential take-away from "flipping the course," which is valuable for all of us, is intentional thinking about what you expect your students to do outside of the classroom in preparation for best learning in the classroom.

Experiential Learning and Community Engagement

Experiential learning refers to learning opportunities that directly engage the student, usually outside the classroom. Internships, co-ops, service learning, student teaching, capstones, and other independent projects are typical formats for experiential learning. Experiential learning can occur in a course format as well, since it generally means hands-on, active learning, which can be accomplished by a variety of means.

Your experiential aspects of the course may be prescribed, as is the case if you are teaching seminars for an internship course, or running an internship course, or they may be subscribed as in the case if you are using various active learning techniques and tools in what might otherwise be a regular "lecture" course.

Your course does not have to be entirely community engagement through "external" learning. Arguably, your community engagement component already occurs to a certain degree in you being an adjunct, in effect from the community, rather than from the "regular" faculty. Engagement can also occur through sending your students out into the community for data gathering and projects, or through bringing members of the community in as interviewees and guests. In courses where we have had final student projects, we have often used the community as review panels for presentations. In such cases, we give them basic rubrics so there is some structure to the reviews. Students tend to work harder on their presentations and projects when they know someone other than the professor will be viewing them. This also models the portfolio aspect of having students prepare for a world of professional practice where they will be expected to have examples of their work products. Again, explaining to the students the reasons for doing this will help their "buy-in" to your community engagement approach.

Assessment Learning

Assessment learning is one of the most used instructional strategies. It is a type of learning that involves students checking their knowledge or understanding through some form of testing. Graded tests, quizzes, exams, papers, or projects are all considered assessment learning. And while this type of learning has received criticism for being overly punitive, assessment learning remains an effective though not necessarily efficient strategy.

There is a certain pressure associated with an activity counting toward a final grade versus an activity for creating a basic understanding. It is for this reason that many professors start off a class period with a graded quiz. This serves multiple purposes. It raises the expectation that students come to class prepared. If administered at the beginning of class, it creates an expectation to arrive on time. If written correctly, it also creates critical thinking opportunities.

In classes where a final exam is heavily weighted, regular, graded, in-class testing is also advantageous. This is especially true if in-class quizzes model questions that are likely to be on exams. It reduces stress and provides students with familiarity on how you make exams. As mentioned in a previous chapter, these quizzes may be low stakes, representing a small percentage of the final total grade. However, it is often important that they be graded assessments. There is a psychological importance to making assessments count for students. Also, make sure to assess concepts that are most important for students to learn and/or concepts that are most difficult to understand. Do not just use throwaway multiple-choice questions that only test memory.

Of course, there is always nuance when it comes to understanding assessment learning, so we will clarify more in the following.

Formative and Summative Assessment

To be effective and efficient in teaching and learning we need to be strategic and tactical in our use of assessments. This means thinking about appropriate deployment of formative and summative assessment. When we first became adjuncts, we had little idea what these terms meant. Summative and formative assessment is academic-speak for figuring out if students know stuff. It is terminology you are not likely to use outside of academia but useful in making the bridge to teaching. Formative assessment is frequent ongoing checking of student progress and student understanding so you can figure out what they need and adjust what you do (Cox 2017). Think of formative assessment as when it isn't too late for the assessment to do some good for the student's learning. Think of summative as final—summing up all of the scores and determining the final average and grade. It tends to be after the student is done learning (i.e., when it is too late).

Gooblar (2019) describes formative assessment as that which is done to influence future performance and summative assessment as measuring past performance. Summative grades for a course are the final grades. Summative assessment has its place, as in exams for professional licenses and other achievements of benchmark competencies. Two reasonable justifications for summative assessment in academia are that it uses benchmarks to build on and that it exists in the outside world.

Formative assessments can be so embedded in the course activities that the student is almost unaware of it as assessment. This is enhanced further if the student sees activities as a means to keep them engaged in a way that lets both them and their instructor check their progress and understanding. The instructor can make it clear the purpose includes identifying learning needs and adjusting teaching appropriately (Cox 2017). This checking is essentially a reinforcing or scaffolding assessment. We monitor student understanding so that students are always aware of their academic strengths and learning gaps when they have opportunities to improve and understand continuously (if they choose to do so).

Exams are not just for summative assessments. Research has established that the very act of taking a test helps students retain class materials superior to students who are not tested (Gooblar 2019). Low-stake tests are less stressful, and tests can be built into a variety of gamelike learning activities. As a prospective instructor, take note that writing good tests and exams is a bit of an art form. Open-ended questions are easy to write but hard to grade. In terms of grading, multiple choice exams are easier and faster to grade but the longer assignments are sometimes better for student learning. Multiple choice exams do take more work upfront to prepare. Many introductory course textbooks for popular subjects come with websites of test banks you can access. But you need to go over those questions and be sure they meet your objectives. It is possible to design multiple choice questions that test higher order thinking, but it is challenging to do so. Also make sure to help your students know how to take exams. It seems obvious, but students forget effective strategies such as using effective learning strategies, rewriting notes, making practice exam questions, setting study times and partners, and so on (see McGuire and McGuire 2015, 117–118 for test-taking strategies and advice, and remind students to visit their campus learning center).

Assessments to Match Course Objectives

When considering the use of assessments, consider that probably the first thing students will seek out is how many exams and what they count for. This is your opportunity to articulate your evaluation strategy, including how you will assess them, and how many "points" the assessment counts for. It is also a good opportunity to explain why you will use the assessments you use. For example, if your course objectives include being able to write technical reports, then having them prepare a technical report is perhaps a better assessment tool than a written exam. The chief reason being it is a logical matchup with the objective. And perhaps explain why that particular objective is there in the first place. A good reason for that objective might be because people in the profession represented by that course are often expected to write or review technical reports. You can provide a rubric for how you will evaluate the technical report, and match this with your course expectations. You can find many models of rubrics for particular topic assessments, but you will most likely want to assemble your own, designed for transparency of grading criteria and ease of grading, perhaps in a checklist form. We have found success with rubrics that contain checklists with columns for the students to assess their own (or peer's) performances in addition to a column for us, the instructors.

Homework and Problem Sets

According to William and Mary's Training and Technical Assistance Center, homework and out-of-classroom practice are effective instructional strategies, helping students to retain content (William and Mary

2019). As former engineering students, homework in the form of the graded problem set or "P-Set" was and still is one of the most widely used forms of assessment in our curricula. We recall that problem sets would count up to 40 percent of our final grade! Homework, whether graded or not, is especially important in the STEM fields where definitions and concepts must transfer from short-term to long-term memory and where repetition is essential for carrying out deeper learning and skill in mastering difficult concepts. Consider homework to be the ultimate form of outside practice. As Dean et al. say, "practice must tightly align with learning objectives and provide students with opportunities to deepen their understanding or become faster and more proficient at a skill" (Dean, Hubbell, Pitler, and Stone 2012, 110).

As you plan your homework strategy, think of the issues and topics of primary concern, your strategy for their learning modes, and the classroom or individual discussions that you hope to spark. These all inform your choice of mode of evaluation. Also think about multiple forms that accommodate a variety of student needs and abilities within a reasonable frame. And as with in-class practice, consider mixing lower stakes homework problems with higher stakes ones to boost confidence.

Plagiarism

Just a brief note on plagiarism. Some students have the perspective that everything is so widespread now and easily accessible, it's not seen as plagiarism. Information is thus seen as "free." And if a question has already been answered on the internet, then many students think they do not have to independently answer that question because it is easily available online. Your assessments, exams or homework, need to be designed to assess true student learning rather than their ability to cut and paste the work of others. Keep in mind that virtually all institutions expect faculty to have some sort of statement about plagiarism and original work in the syllabus.

ChatGPT and Friends

Yes, OpenAI's ChatGPT will likely be a silent member of your class roster, so you might as well prepare for it. There can be other members as well—Bard, Ernie Bot, Bing Chat, Llama 2, Grok; the list is growing. ChatGPT launched on November 22, 2022, as an AI system free for anyone to use. Even us, we have tried it out.

There is very little you can do to design homework that can be totally safe from ChatGPT (Scott 2023). Do you accept AI as a partner in the educational process? Do we use more pencil and paper assessments in class? Do you want to give grades to an AI product? Do we use an AI checker like ZeroGPT? Do we design the use of AI in our papers as in helping the students organize thoughts, make outlines, create drafts? So yes, more questions than answers. Look for academic institutions to be wrestling with these questions. You can assume that there will be a fair amount of deference to individual faculty decisions on this matter. Hopefully, with at least some guidance from your academic department or center for teaching.

Meanwhile, D'Angostino (2023) provides several strategies, which include:

1. Get familiar with AI.
2. Consider traditional human-centric modes of teaching and learning.
3. Ask big questions about the use of AI in course objectives.
4. Think ahead, especially about how your students may be using AI in the future.
5. You don't have to solve all the AI problems. Other departments, offices, administrators, and faculty can help.
6. Assess what ChatGPT can do. What are its failings? Get the students involved in this.
7. Involve students in the conversation about AI.
8. Experiment. Make it low stakes. Try something and if it doesn't work, try something else.

D'Angostino also reminds us not to panic. Don't let the students sense fear. In our experimentation with ChatGPT (we had to play around with it to speak intelligently about it in this book), we have found that it can be useful for creating paper and chapter outlines, for summarizing information found in electronic documents and websites, and even for getting you unstuck when trying to write something new. However, we have also found that the writing it produces can often be very vague, simplistic, and not really say much with significant depth. You inevitably must discard, severely edit, or just use the essence of what the AI bot churned out. You most definitely won't be able to cut and paste without it being obvious. (Though some studies have found that non-native speakers produce writing similar to what AI produces, and incorrectly get accused of using AI.) So, there actually is a benefit to having the students use generative AI as a tool, but with caveats. When we allow students to use calculators, we also clarify by having them "show their work." Something similar should be done with ChatGPT (and friends).

Group Learning

We have discussed group learning previously as something you might want to plan as a teaching strategy. There are pedagogical advantages of group work in enhancing learning outcomes. And yes, group work might seem like it is easier to the instructor because there tends to be less projects to grade. But group work creates more work for the instructor in terms of planning, organizing, and managing. Orchestrating successful group work is an achievement indeed. But students in the work world will need to be prepared for group work and it is reasonable to expect you, an adjunct representing the work world, to be able to prepare your students to be effective team members.

As an adjunct, you might be feeling reluctant to tackle the social dynamics and potential troubles of group work. But with just a little background you might find it a powerful tool to master in helping your students meet your course objectives. It can be particularly useful when you have large enrollments and need some way to make final projects be manageable for you.

Most instructors sooner or later find it advantageous to have their students do group work. Likely you are doing it for sound pedagogical reasons to enhance "learning outcomes" rather than because you might think it will save you time. It is pretty hard to have a professional job and not have to do some group work, so it is good preparation for your students. Further, most students will have encountered group work and expect to have more of it in their education. Group work can help students learn in class and outside of class; it can help build community (Bain 2004). You can set it up in a manner that is not overly stressful and that makes the students not feel they are giving away control of their own grade to other students.

Students in groups can review each other's work and provide constructive criticism. At the end of a major project rather than have students in a group grade each other have them evaluate the amount and quality of their own work. You might also have them estimate the amount of work others in their group were doing. You can allow peer comments on other students (constructive suggestions/assessment) or even have them evaluate the quality of work of others in their group.

Be sure they know everyone is doing whatever method you choose, by being sure it is in the syllabus. Well, who are we kidding—they are not going to read that. Make a separate handout. Call it a Group Project Rubric because that sounds educational/official and objective. Also announce this in class periodically. The math for this approach is not hard—if you have two students and they each claim to do 50 percent of the work that tells you something. Four students in a group and one claims they did 75 percent of the work, you have a good idea someone might have been shirking (or someone was overreaching). You will probably find that students are used to self-assessment and appreciate the opportunity to do it.

If you decide to have students work in groups because you think you will have less grading to do, and that it will make less work overall for you, you are wrong. But it was a good idea on your part, and you tried. At least, there are side benefits. Most jobs have collaborative aspects to them, and it is important to get your students socialized to the point where they can actually cooperate with one another. Group work helps promote the idea of individual responsibility and acknowledging the work of others.

Large classes sometimes mean you need projects and other assignments to be done in groups because you cannot grade 150 of them by yourself. Some students will be frustrated that their individual work is affected and not adequately recognized. You can explain that group work is a requirement of many jobs. This is especially palatable coming from you as an adjunct who is out there in the working world bringing expertise to the class. You can design your assessments to address these and similar concerns by having progress reports and other related deliverables.

Handling Personalities Within Groups

We previously mentioned various types of students from a classroom perspective (Chapter 3). Others have done this sorting from the perspective of students who work on team assignments. For example, Elizabeth Hoyt (2019) describes five types of students in the context of group projects. She aims her advice at students to help them respond to the increased amount of group work in academia, which is fair, because much of the work world involves group projects.

For each type, Hoyt provides a "how to handle the situation." The "invisible student" is more apt to need faculty intervention. First, have the group assign this person small, measurable, concrete tasks that are time-dependent and thus pull him or her into the rest of the group. The invisible student depends on the work of others. The "silent student" also tends to do this. But the group at least has a better chance to draw him or her out through specific, but nonthreatening, questions and actions. Hoyt's third type, the procrastinator, is universal. Helping that person recognize and manage deadlines to build incrementally toward success is key.

The overpromise/underdeliver person may have modulation problems. Again, the incremental approach is useful and clearly linking deliverables with due dates and periodic check-ins. Hoyt recommends positive feedback, or, with care, constructive criticism. However, the typical college student is, chronologically, an adult and likely quite aware of overpromising and underdelivering and thus rather sensitive to any criticism. It may be best to just shrug and say "those are the rules."

For control freaks, Hoyt advises appreciating that they at least care, and letting them know you share the seriousness of the matter and are willing to pitch in. Control freaks are apt to be overachievers and will appreciate sharing the burden on team projects. The danger is when the load gets too uneven. Everybody knows the experience of being in a group where at least one member rides on the coat-tails of others. One wonders whether the overachiever gains from carrying the bulk of the load, but at least we can say they are preparing for the real world.

Some categories reveal themselves in the classroom by posture and lack of action ("the slacker"; arguably a form of procrastinator) or by behavior, such as the "Uber-boss" (a particular type of control freak). We do not recommend sharing those terms, especially in public. Do not confuse the student types (invisible student, slacker, etc.) with group task titles, nor assign them as labels or titles to members of the group. At least not in print or out loud.

A useful strategy is to remind groups of the stages in the process articulated by Tuckman: the forming, storming, norming, and performing (Tuckman 1965). There is plenty of additional literature on group process models, but these first four are sufficient for our purposes in working with student groups in the classroom. Students who know of these stages experience less frustration than others, as they can envision how the whole process will work (or at least theoretically might).

Okay, so those are the stages in the process. If the group knows about them, it can begin to accommodate them and keep momentum. Students can also better appreciate how group work is a manageable process. Within the process there are tools we can use to advance the group project or assignment. One of these tools is to approach group work from a people management perspective. Groups work better when members have task-oriented roles. The tasks can be specific duties or general categories. We recommend fostering group work by assigning task-based categories to students. As an adjunct representing "the real world" in the classroom, students will appreciate you bringing this structured professional approach to the class.

In addition to the formal task categories, use incremental deadlines for check-ins and "deliverables." This is what they will have to do in the "real world." You can build these into the syllabus. Assign points (credit) to them so the students take them seriously. Have some assessments in the process so students evaluate the amount and quality of their work in the group (if not also that of the others in their group).

Some Tips for Group Work

1. Foster team spirit from the beginning. Start with get-to-know-you activities.
2. Focus on the positive aspects of teamwork. Have groups consciously incorporate the positive aspects of teamwork in every team activity.
3. Minimize interpersonal conflicts. If you already know the students, split up close friends/couples as much as possible when assigning them to groups.
4. Clearly define the responsibilities of each team member and their roles (recorder, task manager, researcher, data manager, archivist, etc.) in writing. Have team members write out and sign a work contract regarding fair division of labor and individual responsibilities.
5. Use built-in progress reports. Make these gradable items. Continually monitor the progress of the project before things crash.
6. Increase communication within and outside the classroom.
7. Escape clause: Give groups the option to change teams under special circumstances with instructor consent. Be careful with this too, as there are consequences.

8. Reward for individual accountability, also rewards for the team when the entire team performs well. Individual credit given at instructor's discretion.

9. Choose a random presenter from each group for group presentations. That way, every member of the group has to be equally prepared.

Teaching Tips From the K-12 (and Beyond) Crowd

You do not have time or opportunity for all the teaching assistance colleges and universities may offer. You may not be versed in your formal education or experience on neuroscience or how people learn. Yet as an adjunct you already know you have to be particularly effective and efficient. One way to achieve this is to look at what the experts do. Teachers in the K-12 world are experts in how students learn because they have had specific coursework and extensive experience in doing that.

K-12 Tips

Here are some major reasons to look at what K-12 teachers do and see what you can exploit or appropriate for your course:

1. Teachers have had courses in education, and experience applying what they've learned.

2. Teachers are used to a collaborative model of sharing and helping each other, certainly more so than the more individualistic nature of the professoriate in higher education. Many teachers post information, activities, lesson plans, and resources online for anyone to use.

3. There are many more people in K-12 education than in higher education. Since there are more of them there is much more to borrow from.

4. Frankly, there is not that much difference between younger students and college students. People are people.

5. The few differences that do exist between K-12 students and college students often means teachers have had to deal with a wider range of challenges, thereby gaining greater experience.

6. The many regulations, forms, assessments, and other imposed obligations and restrictions that K-12 teachers deal with lead them to seek ever more efficient means of getting learning accomplished in the precious time allotted for that.

7. Odds are great that your college students were once K-12 students and thus have some experience with the methods and approaches used by K-12 teachers. What you borrow from them will not be alien to your students.

8. Teachers appreciate the connection to higher education since they went to college too and they are interested in students as lifelong learners. They may appreciate reciprocation in terms of your possibly (or rather presumably, we hope) more advanced knowledge within your own field as a working professional.

9. You likely had a K-12 teacher who made a great difference in your education and whom you will never forget.

Of course, good advice also comes from undergraduate instructors who deal with concerns more relatable to lectures and condensed meeting times, so here we provide some tips mostly from K-12 and end with some from higher education.

"Dipsticks" to Gauge Learning

These are based on Todd Finley's 2014 article published by *Edutopia* (a very useful resource that we have used extensively in our college instruction). Following are a few that work well in college. These are just a handful of the many hundreds of alternative formative assessments that can help students learn to assess their own understanding:

- List 10 key words from an assigned text.
- Explain the main idea using an analogy.

- Identify the theory or idea the author is advancing. Then identify an opposite theory. What are the similarities and differences between these ideas?
- What frustrates and confuses you about the text? Why?
- Draw a picture that illustrates a relationship between terms in the text. Explain in one paragraph your visual representation.
- Create a two-column table. Use the left column to write down five to eight important quotations. Use the right column to record reactions to the quotations.
- Describe how you solved an academic problem, step by step.
- Color Cards: Red = "Stop, I need help." Green = "Keep going, I understand." Yellow = "I'm a little confused."

The 5E Instructional Method

One example of a useful approach for active learning brought to higher education from K-12 is the 5E instructional method (Gooblar 2019). Use this approach as you plan your class session. Each class period should use the cycle of 5E:

- Engagement. Short interaction that "hooks" the student on the topic
- Exploration. Hands-on activity on the topic or lesson
- Explanation. Analyze the topic and their understanding of it
- Elaboration. New application and context for the topic
- Evaluation. Assess student learning

Other "Hacks"

These are very useful tricks that will get you through some trouble spots, especially when handling disruptions or feeling like you are falling flat in front of the crowd:

- "Get quiet, not loud." Regardless of age, audiences will get loud and rowdy if left to their own devices. There is an urge to start yelling at the group, but an even more effective approach is to start whispering or to go completely quiet. It does not take long for the group to realize that you are just standing in the front staring at them.

- "Watch yourself teach." Take out your smartphone and film yourself teaching. Play it back and take notes on your performance. You may be surprised by what you find.
- Use an anonymous discussion board. All learning management systems have built-in discussion boards. You can use them as a platform for students to ask questions, questions they may think are silly or that make them sound unintelligent. Usually, you can set the board to anonymous posting for other students (but you are able to view who posted what in case someone goes off the rails).

Beyond K-12

1. **Tips for fostering deep learning**

Edna Ross (2021) gives her top six "tips for fostering deep learning in person and online."

- Take and track attendance. Count attendance and participation in course grade.
- Start class with a question that activates previous knowledge.
- "Reset the clock" with polling questions. Do this every 7 to 10 minutes.
- Pose open-ended questions and have students discuss results. Pull scientific (critical) thinking into the discussion.
- Create on-screen "action" so there are not just static slides and whiteboards.
- Ask closing questions for each session. Summarize responses. Use discussion boards and announcements. Exit poll on muddiest point.

2. **Making lectures more engaging and interactive**

Perhaps the most satisfying feeling for a lecturer is the feeling when a class period just "clicks" for them. They have somehow stumbled upon the intersection of engaging subject matter, engaged students, a great presentation pace, funny jokes, great examples, an ability to answer questions that the students raise, and a "wrap up" of the lecture that ends right on time. This is what we call a "unicorn" class period. It is awesome when it happens, and it is rare for most. But there are techniques and strategies that you can consider trying to increase the regularity of a unicorn class period. These inevitably involve a mix of inquiry-based learning and teacher-directed instruction. Youki Terada laid out a useful list in a recent article, "8 Evidence-Based Tips to Make Your Lectures More Engaging—and Memorable." They are as follows:

- Review background knowledge (of the students)
- Take breaks
- Check for student understanding during class time
- Slow down
- Record your lectures
- Incorporate visual aids and graphic organizers
- Relate the work to your students' lives
- Be authentic in your conversational style

3. **When teaching once a week**

Many part-timers find themselves teaching a course that meets once a week, often at an uncomfortable time slot for students. It is particularly important for such classes to break up the session. Learning is improved by having breaks or intervals (Carey 2014). Consider using three stages, with breaks in between for long classes. Three possible divisions:

1. Unload content via lecture, handouts, and interactions. One-third of class time.
2. Active learning by small groups or as individuals. One-third or more of class time.

3. Come back to a large group/entire class—report out, synthesis, processing, redirect, assessment, feedback, building class community. One-third or less of class time.

Conclusion

Better teaching means engaging the student with active learning. Think out your teaching activities that implement the learning objectives you developed in your syllabus. The more inclusive your teaching is, the more likely you are to connect with all students in your class. Designing your course with multiple sorts of activities, assignments, and engagements will help your class be inclusive. Your active teaching will encourage students to realize their learning potentials, which means increasing their metacognition about learning.

There are many tools and methods you can use in the classroom. Some of the best of them come from the K-12 world, so do not be afraid to look at and borrow what you remember from your own education and what you see from the best K-12 teachers. Many of them actively post and share materials online. Your colleagues will be doing this as well. The CTL at your institution will capture many of the best examples and provide them to you along with workshops and training on how to use them.

Your students will be aware of tricks and tools that can improve their own learning, or at least their test scores. You need to be aware of some of these and co-opt them as needed. For example, ChatGPT and AI are rising "stars." They are not going away anytime soon. Nor will attendant issues such as plagiarism. So you need to figure out how to incorporate the use of assistive tools and AI in a positive fashion, or at least how to help your students deal with them. You will need to help your students understand the nuances and dangers of plagiarism in their academic careers, and the potential resultant reflection on their careers.

You will hear about "flipping the classroom" and other ways to help students get the most out of classroom time. You will be making decisions about what tools can help and what can get in the way. You will be gaining familiarity with formative and summative assessments. As an adjunct you may have an opportunity for formal training and workshops like your full-time colleagues, but you will likely have much less time than them to take advantage of these opportunities. So you will have to be strategic and seek out CTL functions geared toward adjuncts, and online resources you can pursue on your own time at an as-needed basis.

The variety of methods and tools briefly mentioned here should give you a good start in preparing for active teaching and learning. Consult some of the references we've provided and you will get even more good ideas. Your academic department and CTL will likely be only too eager to hear of your interest in teaching tools and tips, so reach out to them if you do not already see something of interest. Continue to monitor online self-paced and in-person workshops from the CTL. This will have the added benefit of getting you known to other faculty and support staff as someone interested in teaching and learning.

You are not alone in this mission; so look to your colleagues, and think back on what you've learned from the best K-12 teachers. If you are teaching an introductory textbook with a major book publisher, there likely is a great deal of useful information already available from them. The LMS is designed to support commonly used tools for teaching and assessment.

As we wrap up this chapter, here are a few recommendations for teaching during and after a class session from an article titled "Tips for Faculty Teaching for the First Time" from the CTL of Washington University in Saint Louis (2024):

- Interact with students and include opportunities for active learning. Students want to feel that you are not just talking at them. They want you to take interest in what they are thinking. Even in a lecture, pause periodically to ask questions, or to ask students to solve a problem or discuss a point.
- There will be good teaching days and not-so-good days in the classroom, so be flexible. If your teaching strategy is not working that day, try something else. Give a pop quiz. Start a small group discussion. Anything to get you out of that rut.

- Take notes on how the class went. Note what worked and what didn't, as well as any new ideas that occurred to you while teaching. Make any necessary adjustments to your plan for the next class session. Do you need to make changes in the way that you present material? Is there anything you can do to improve student participation?

Finally, hang on to your reasons for teaching. They will help keep you motivated.

CHAPTER 6

On Learning

Introduction

This chapter delves into learning, debunking prevalent myths and highlighting evidence-based realities. This could easily be a book on its own so we are just going to give you highlights of what may be most useful to know as a contingent professor. By understanding the nature of learning, educators can craft learning strategies that resonate with students and foster meaningful, lasting knowledge acquisition.

Likely you will hear about "learning styles" if you have not already, particularly from students. Not that you want to confront them, but the notion of learning styles has been thoroughly debunked in the literature (Brown and Kaminske 2018), and a teaching focus on them may even be detrimental to the learning community when it interferes with developing a rounded set of needed skills and abilities. Researchers have failed to find a correlation between learning styles and successful learning. What are these learning styles anyway? Essentially, learning styles have been differentiated based on visual, aural, kinesthetic, verbal, mathematical, interpersonal (group learning), and intrapersonal (learning alone). But we hear a great deal about learning styles. Is there anything good in considering them?

Felder (2010) argues for the validity of learning styles, reminding us that they are a set of tendencies. Naturally, we all recognize the existence of sets of tendencies. Some of us even have our own tendencies. Like we prefer to learn by doing, or by watching others, or by reading, or, our personal preference, by making mistakes; "fail fast, fail cheap" as entrepreneur Doug Hall repeatedly says (2007). Benjamin (2017) states for innovators that "learn fast, learn cheap" is a much better mantra, but that is another story.

Anyway, Felder summarizes components of learning styles, such as *sensing* versus *intuition* and *concrete* versus *abstract*. He notes that it is simply not possible to teach all students in their preferred manner. Fortunately, this meshes with the simple fact that to be successful in any profession students need "attributes associated with all learning style categories" (Felder 2010, 3). We can employ a variety of learning tendencies in our teaching and learning within a single class (Brown and Kaminske 2018). At the very least, this nurtures those abilities in students and keeps us alert. This is why we reframe this subject matter as learning *preferences*.

Teaching to specific preferences is much less important than possessing and employing good communication skills, which includes presenting the information in multiple ways that offers the student many opportunities and modes of learning. This is in accordance with universal design for learning (UDL) principles (Burgstahler 2013). All faculty should be familiar with UDL at least for this reason if not for the importance of helping students with disabilities. Good communication includes providing multiple modes of learning without categorizing into learning preferences. In doing so, we seek to present information in more than one way. We use intentional (reinforcing) redundancy, mixing text with figures, talking, and other modes. We ask, "How can I explain this in a way that will make sense to the student?"

Categorizing the individual can lead to the assumption of fixed or rigid learning patterns, which can impair motivation for students to apply themselves or to adapt. Systematic studies have found little to no evidence supporting the idea that matching material to fit certain learning preferences is effective in educational success. Students will learn by thinking about how they learn not because the material was changed to fit their most comfortable method to learn a subject. This is especially important for the adjunct teaching a large (50 to a 100 or more) student course section. It is simply not possible to accommodate individual preferences. Fortunately, the data says it is not beneficial to do so.

Jarrett (2015) suggests that students should adapt class material into formats that fit how they learn rather than professors trying to modify the class to fit the learning preferences of their students. Thus, students personalize the learning by taking it into their own hands. This can lead to some interesting products, such as transforming the material into songs, drawings, skits, or whatever they think best supports their learning. But it requires the student to take ownership of the learning process, which has become much more difficult in the era of a consumer-orientation to most services.

Debunking Popular Learning Myths

We have already discussed learning styles myths in the introduction, but there are a few other myths that the contingent professor should be familiar with.

The Learning Pyramid Myth

We continue to be fascinated by this obsession over the concept of the learning pyramid. The more we read about it the more we find that it is more folklore than evidence based. A good background is given in a recent open access article "Excavating the origins of the learning pyramid myths" by Letrud and Hernes (2018). The authors explain how the Learning Pyramid "enjoys a considerable level of authority within several areas of educational studies, despite that nobody knows how they originated or whether they were supported by any empirical evidence." The pyramid model predates most empirical research into the field of education studies and learning psychology.

According to the Learning Pyramid, one retains little from hearing or attending lectures, which is usually depicted as the tip of the pyramid and representing little usefulness. Reading is next and is almost equally inefficient, according to the myth. Seeing something, as in viewing a film or a demonstration, helps a learner retain more, while talking, participating in discussions, having direct experiences, practicing, and teaching others are extremely efficient for learning and retention.

We humans have a false intuitive feeling that this is true, so we don't question it. (Humans have gotten into trouble with this bug/feature embedded in our programming.) But what's worse is the models often place percentages on the effects on retention in increments of 5 or 10 percent. For instance, 10 percent retention for attending lectures to 90 percent retention for teaching others. This is a good reason to be skeptical about the pyramid; those numbers are too exact and often accompanied by no empirical data.

It turns out that the whole enterprise of attributing percentages to learning styles and pervading modern academic literature comes from Treichler, an affiliate with Mobil Oil Company (later ExxonMobil), who published these numbers in the late 1960s. Further excavations by Letrud and Hernes and others link similar claims between 1852 and 1901, revealing more about the pyramid hierarchy than actual percentages, with no evidence of corroborating research.

Evidence of a quantification seems to have come from Reverend Charles Roads, 1906. According to Letrud and Hernes, "Roads discusses the pedagogical usefulness of having large illustrations from the Bible on the wall of the Sunday school's main room." Roads places numbers (fractions actually) to his thinking based on his personal experiences! Letrud and Hernes conclude that the field of learning psychology is at least 20 years younger than the model itself.

Bottom line: If you hear or see "literature" about the learning pyramid, be skeptical of it. Focus on evidence-based learning strategies to help your students be successful. We will discuss essential ones at the end of the chapter.

The Multitasking Myth

The college classroom is a minefield of distraction. After years of restricted device use during class time in grade school and high school, college students are now allowed and sometimes encouraged to use all sorts of devices in the lecture hall. There are no mobile phone restriction policies at the university level. If professors have personal policies, sometimes they are viewed as draconian, and they are not easily enforceable. Laptops and tablets are used to take notes. WiFi connections create the ability to surf the net and stream movies all while listening to the professor and "learning" about upper-level topics that often require focus and attention. Layered on top of all this is that modern students have been sold on the idea that multitasking is a productivity hack, and that they are way better at it than previous generations. This can lead to trouble for them.

One of our favorite web articles and the subject of one of our more popular podcast episodes when we were actively producing them is on the myth of multitasking, published and routinely updated on *Psychology Today* (Moralis and Dinan 2022) and based on the work of Rubenstein and co-workers (2001). Multitasking, according to the article, is defined as the act of completing more than one task at the same time, like studying for a test while making lunch, or doing homework problems while streaming Netflix. In fact, in these examples we are not doing anything simultaneously. We are indeed switching back and forth between two (often three or four) tasks.

Our cerebral cortex (the part responsible for thinking, planning, memory, etc.) needs to alternate between goal shifting and rule activation in order to do parallel activities. According to Rubenstein, our brain will turn off the rules for the previous activity and turn on the rules for the new one depending on the goal. This switching costs time and, in turn, focus, accuracy, and awareness. It is a disaster for students who are already easily distracted by push notifications on their mobile devices.

Bottom line: Those who say they are great at multitasking are probably fooling themselves. There is good evidence to suggest to students that they should leave their phones off while in class and that they should limit their laptop use. Better yet, take some of our teaching tips in Chapter 5 and create a class setting that makes students work on activities that do not require devices to complete them. Additionally, build activities that are time sensitive, that reduce the need to divert their attention, and that place firm and reasonable expectations for completion in that allotted time.

Left Brain Versus Right Brain Learning Myth

Many people will erroneously say they need to use their right-brain hemisphere for certain usually creative tasks and their left-brain hemisphere for other more analytical tasks. If you do a basic internet search, you will be bombarded with web pages, books, videos, social media posts, and creativity tests all pushing this concept as real science. Some "learning styles" authors even reference left brain/right brain differences (UArkansas 2024). So, it should not be surprising to hear this even in college hallways.

The left/right brain learning myth has roots in the work performed by Robert Sperry, a Cal Tech neuroscientist working in the 1960s and 1970s with sick epileptics seeking relief from their ailment (UArkansas 2024). In that work, Sperry and a team of surgeons performed drastic procedures that would remove the corpus callosum, which connects the two hemispheres of the brain. While relieving epileptic seizures, the procedure also revealed to Sperry and colleagues that cognitive differences existed based on hemisphere. Unfortunately, this information got extrapolated to an oversimplified explanation related to left/right brain dominance and artistic or analytical personality types and learning preferences. "Right brain–left brain" should be considered more as a figure of speech than anything else (Shmerling 2022; Wharton 2023).

This narrative is another in a long line of "logical" oversimplifications that humans use to better understand themselves and to develop methods and protocols to be more productive. So, while it is true that certain functions reside more on one hemisphere, our brains need both hemispheres to work together to function properly and learn new concepts and skills. There is no such thing as right brain and left-brain learning.

Understanding How Learning Works

There are many ways to think about learning. It is often linked to personality and temperament. The educational literature is rife with all types of models. Let us show you how easy it is to get into the weeds. Golay (1982), taking a Jungian approach to learning as a correlation of personality types, suggested that learning is divided into actual and conceptual, and further divided into spontaneous, routine, specific, and global. He suggested that about 38 percent of learning is actual spontaneous, 8 percent is actual routine, 12 percent is conceptual specific, and 12 percent is conceptual global. (For those who are Greek-god minded, Kiersey and Bates [1987] termed these, respectively, Dionysian: artisan temperament, Epimethean: guardian temperament, Promethean: rational temperament, and Appolonian: idealist temperament). *Actual spontaneous* refers to direct experience, needing to see. *Actual routine* means structured; *conceptual specific* means classifying and "thinking about." *Conceptual global* means people-oriented, with life as a process of self-discovery. Golay's categories (1982) reflect learners as active agents, routine learners, focused learners, and global learners.

Five major learning theories are cognitive, behavioral learning, constructivist, humanism, and connectivism (WGU 2020). Cognitive learning theory focuses on the way students think. Behavioral learning theory focuses on the way students behave, which is subject to external influences and factors. Constructivism learning theory has to do with how students build previous experiences in an active process of their unique construction of the world. Humanism learning theory is a refinement of constructivism further toward self-actualization of the student as an agent in their learning. Connectivism is one of the newer theories based on how the student builds and perceives connections in their experience and learning.

Other learning theories include transformative, which deals with the transformative aspects of education for the student, and social learning theory, which tends to be used for troubled students concerned with the socialization aspects of learning.

Cognitive Load Theory

Cognitive load theory is about optimizing the amount of information students get so they are challenged but not overwhelmed. What is behind this balancing act? The brain acquires primary knowledge unconsciously, but secondary knowledge—the learning you are trying to get accomplished—happens through initial processing of information into working memory. After that, it gets moved into long-term memory. Once it is in long-term memory, it can be fetched back into working memory for cognitive use in dealing with the environment. The best instructional design procedures are those that reduce demand on working memory load.

Students who learn without being overloaded have less stress and do better at processing information into long-term storage (Plass, Moreno, and Brünken 2010). K-12 teachers are taught this theory and become aware of capacity expectations for their grades, and how to achieve them through appropriate pedagogy. Adjuncts are less likely to have had this preparation and must rely on their own intuition and experience and the advice of others, such as peers in the academic unit and the institution's. The syllabus itself represents a cognitive load "dosing" document that helps you achieve a balance of enough stimuli for your students to get your learning objectives met as effectively as possible. It communicates your approach to the student, whose main concern is likely to be determining the work they must do, and how it will be assessed.

Soliciting student feedback and conducting formative assessments will help the instructor fine-tune their sense of what is appropriate. Educational technology can be used to improve cognitive loading (Sweller 2019). This involves planning out your use of technology and how it best supports your course so that you can reserve equipment and classrooms and make other arrangements to avoid surprises. Use of formative assessments supports cognitive load management (improved "germane" cognitive loading). Metacognitive monitoring of learning and performance can enhance the student's cognitive load (Leppink 2017).

Metacognition

Metacognition is about getting the big picture. It involves thinking about the context for how student learning occurs and how it affects their lives. Ultimately, college students as adults are responsible for their own learning. But they certainly benefit from your guidance in doing this. We know that metacognitive activities and abilities reduce stress, gives students skills for their learning, and improves their cognitive load management. Metacognition need not be taught as a separate tool or skill. In fact, the literature shows it is best learned in the context of specific subjects or tasks (Quigley, Muijs, and Stringer 2021).

When you have students do practice tests and think about or discuss what they learn, you are using one of the most effective metacognitive tools (Dunlosky et al. 2013). Other effective metacognition and self-regulating tools include other practice activities spaced out over time, elaboration by students of why something is true (explanation rather than mere recitation of facts), and self-explanation by students. In self-explanation, the student explains what they are doing and why. This becomes particularly effective in group work. But it also can be encouraged by having students explain their work to the teacher or class. By using these techniques, you are modeling metacognition behavior as a teacher. The students will pick up on this, making it more likely that they incorporate it into their own practice (Quigley, Muijs, and Stringer 2021). It may be useful to state this approach in your syllabus and in the summary of your intended assessments for the course.

When students interact with their materials it is a form of metacognition. This includes things as simple as underlining text or making marginal notes. Use of multiple colors and fonts is also a form of metacognition. Even changing font size benefits metacognition (Chang and Brainerd 2022). This information is great for your students who are doodlers and need something to keep their hands busy. They benefit from finding out that all this is actually a form of metacognition that improves their learning.

Seven Steps to Improve Metacognition

Quigley, Muijs, and Stringer (2021,14) recommend seven steps to teaching students how to improve their metacognition and self-regulation. Do not be intimidated by them, as you can fold them into your regular subject teaching. These steps are as follows:

1. Activating prior knowledge
2. Explicit strategy instruction

3. Modeling of learned strategy

4. Memorization of strategy

5. Guided practice

6. Independent practice

7. Structured reflection

Incorporating the first step in cognition improvement, activating prior knowledge, requires assessing what that prior knowledge is, and dealing with any misconceptions that have occurred in receiving or processing this past knowledge. If you are teaching the first course in a college subject, you have to go back to what the students brought with them from their high school education. If you are teaching a course in a sequence, you need to have an idea of what was covered in the previous course(s) and what will be covered in the subsequent courses so you can adequately prepare your students. Dealing with misconceptions—even thinking out whether or not misconceptions exist is in itself metacognition. Misconceptions occur because of inaccurate information, misinterpretation of information, or some other aspects of faulty reasoning. They can be quite difficult to dispel, but metacognition can help in doing so (Savion 2012).

Metacognition is also an aspect of "deep learning." Ross (2021) provides advice that promotes this. She emphasizes the importance of having students see that you value their attendance and participation. So yes, do take and track attendance. Count attendance and participation in the course grade. She suggests starting each class session with a question that activates previous knowledge—an important linking tool. Periodic check-ins help "reset the clock" by polling questions that get students involved and help them reflect on where they are. Open-ended questions in which students discuss results encourage metacognition. The discussion is advanced whenever critical thinking ("scientific" thinking) is used. For media usage, she calls for on-screen "action" so there are not just static slides and whiteboards. At the end of each class session use closing questions and summarize responses. Discussion boards and announcements can be used to bring the class management systems into it. Students can be given an exit poll on the muddiest point, which contributes to their metacognition and yours.

Many instructors start their course with a list of assumptions they articulate to the students. Some of this can be in the syllabus. This sets the groundwork for metacognition, which can continue with you providing resources for students to follow up on these assumptions. Evaluate which of these assumptions are associated with misconceptions. A discussion of these assumptions helps set a firm foundation for learning; you can see what you need to clear up and what you can already rely on.

Motivation and Learning

Intrinsic motivation is learning for its own sake. It is what Nobel Laureate Richard Feynman called "the pleasure of finding things out" (1999, entitled as such). Intrinsic motivation manifests as thoughtful questions, enthusiasm, active participation and effort (Dagnall 2021).

Extrinsic motivation are all the external influences, such as the desire for good grades, getting a good job, praise, anything other than learning for its own sake. Extrinsic motivation is external rewards for outcomes. The question is how to increase student motivation. This can be done through structured reward systems (exemption from quiz, good grades, other compensation in the course) and through more general situational rewards, such as praise and recognition from peers and faculty. Academic "bribes" are perfectly acceptable. Ideally, we want extrinsic rewards to support a sense of intrinsic reward; to be in sync with the values structure of good learning and the importance of knowledge.

Extrinsic motivators that do not mesh with intrinsic values and motivators can have a negative influence (Bain 2004). However, extrinsic motivators that boost academic performance incline students more favorable toward the subject material and intrinsic factors (Unamba, Onyekwere, and Ekwutosim 2018). Extrinsic motivation leading to student success can contribute to the joy of learning, thus boosting intrinsic motivation.

The learning environment can increase motivation by enhancing the conditions of learning through making "fun," safe and rewarding scenarios for the exchange of information, and the carrying out of assignments and activities. Enough stimuli are provided to engage and challenge students but not so much as to be "high stakes." Thus, the educational environment is seen as valuable and not too risky. Performance criteria and assessment criteria can do this. For example, providing student work from previous semesters that produced an "A" with a promise of scaffolding or formative assessment feedback that can help the student achieve similar levels of performance.

Lifelong Learning and Continuous Education

Think of continuous education as "professional development" and lifelong learning as both formal and informal processes of continuing to find things out. Lifelong learning can be personal or professional. What you do to improve student learning will make a difference that may resonate well beyond your course. Anything that celebrates love of learning will boost intrinsic motivation. An increase in intrinsic motivation will contribute toward success in the classroom and ultimately to a lifeline learning mindset.

Lifelong learning is enhanced by having goals and strategies to achieve them. Simply keeping up with technological change means it is increasingly necessary to be lifelong learners unless you can afford to pay other people to keep up for you. Similarly, professions change much faster than previously. Many have continuing education requirements for membership.

Many large corporations and government agencies encourage a lifelong learner approach. Knowledge Anywhere (2024), a software company that provides a major source of corporate training and corporate LMS, recommends five major strategies that lend themselves well to an academic world: provide mentorship opportunities, provide ongoing employee workshops and webinars, compensate for time spent, give "real" incentives, and provide online courses. If you continue to work in academia, you are likely to need continued training in FERPA (student confidentiality) compliance, student accessibility, teaching methods, research compliance, and other academically related areas. Most institutions are only too happy to provide this to their adjuncts and your most difficult problem may just be in finding the time.

Recent demographic shifts have reflected the trend in education for more "nontraditional" students in the classroom. There is an increase in the use of adjuncts who bring a diverse range of knowledge and approaches to the classroom. There is an increase in the diversity of students as society increases educational opportunities and the need for an educated citizenry. Academic institutions have expanded their recruitment networks for students who seek degrees or merely pursue courses for the sake of learning—true lifelong learners. Creating a positive learning environment increases motivation and increases the chance for students to become "hooked' into being a lifelong learner.

Evidence-Based Learning Practices

It is easy to fall down learning theory rabbit holes, so let us redirect to strategies you can use. Because, ultimately, you want to do what works most effectively to promote student learning. You have to pay attention to time, budget, and technique. So, what works best for learning strategies? What does the evidence show?

Following are six such practices that we have synthesized using web pages from various CTLs. Another excellent resource that has influenced our understanding of learning practices and that you might consider using comes from the Learning Scientists (learningscientists.org), a group of cognitive psychologists focused on evidence-based learning strategies.

Retrieval Practice

According to Washington University in St. Louis, retrieval practice is one of the signature evidence-based learning strategies (WUSTL 2024). In short, retrieval practice is a recall strategy. The act of retrieving facts, concepts, and events from memory strengthens learning. This may seem obvious, but it is amazing how many students claim to know something about a topic or concept but are unable to prove or show that through recall. They often conflate familiarity of a concept with mastery of said concept. Retrieval practice is a technique for the deliberate "jogging" of one's memory until the proper connections are formed for fluency in that subject.

This is why flashcards work so well—they strengthen the connections in your memory each time you practice recall from them. Note that these days many students use online apps like Quizlet instead of physical flashcards, but the idea is the same even though increasing evidence suggests that handwritten notes strengthen memorization and deeper learning more than when done with typing and screens. Either way, there is a large body of evidence supporting that retrieval practice outperforms repeated studying (reading over and over again) or even concept mapping.

In addition to flashcards, Washington University suggests incorporating into your class low-stakes recall quizzes, "two-things" memory jogs, and one-page in-class "brain dumps" with discussion to get students used to accessing long- and short-term memory.

Spaced Practice

According to Indiana University (IU) Bloomington, spaced practice is a learning technique that utilizes rest periods between practice periods (IU-Bloomington 2024). It has an equivalent effect to incorporating rest days when lifting physical weights to promote muscle growth. By allowing students to let information "soak in" and routinely revisit after short breaks (on the order of days or a week), it will improve memory retention over longer periods, even when the actual hours of learning are the same. Though not exactly equivalent to our muscles recovering from the lifting of heavy weights, our brains do need time to move information from working memory to long-term memory. Indeed, many business groups now use this knowledge for more effective training of personnel.

This again makes intuitive sense if you think about the opposite of spaced practice, which we know as "cramming." Many students use the strategy that they will study nonstop for 12 to 24 hours the day before a big test or final exam and cram as much information into their short-term memory as possible just in time for completing the final exam. Though some people are effective at using the cramming strategy to achieve the short-term goal of passing a test, it is widely accepted that this practice results in almost complete loss of long-term memory retention.

Implementation strategies suggested by IU Bloomington include giving repeated attempts at the same quiz but separated by a few days or a week, use question banks to draw random questions of the same topic to reinforce in slightly different ways, and return to earlier concepts throughout the semester either through written activities or clicker questions. These are helpful if you are teaching a class that uses summative evaluation.

Interleaving Practice

According to the University of Arizona UA Learning Initiative, "interleaving" is where learners mix, or interleave, multiple subjects or topics while they study (UA 2024). This is the opposite of the very common method of blocked study, where students will study one subject in a longer block of time before moving on to the next subject. This to many is counterintuitive, but according to researchers, interleaving forces the brain to continually retrieve information from deeper memory because each practice attempt is interleaved with other unrelated subjects. Retrieval is different from the last attempt, so rote memorization from short-term memory will not work if what is in short-term memory is an entirely different topic.

Interleaving is most beneficial if topics are related somehow. For example, interleaving mathematics, physics, and chemistry and cycling through the subjects in one session may be beneficial, especially when working on quantification. If your subject matter relates to other classes that they are taking, whether in other departments or in their major courses for a given semester, you can integrate questions on how what they are learning in your class relates to other subjects they are currently studying. In fact, it is helpful to get a sense of what other classes your students are taking during that semester to see if you can provide extra opportunities to work with those subjects within the context of your course. It helps you be more relatable to the students, and it shows them that there are real connections between what they are studying in other classes and what you are teaching them.

There is also an advantage of mixing different forms of practice to improve learning (Shatz 2024). For example, if you have students practice multiple types of questions for an exam (essay versus quantification versus conceptualizing), that is "interleaving." However, a caveat of using interleaving is that you should not use it when learning is becoming taxing. You shouldn't jump to another subject when the concept in the one you are currently studying is suddenly too hard or confusing or if the critical thinking question is taking more time than a few definitions or multiple-choice concept questions. Work through that challenge before moving on to another subject or modality within the interleaving study period.

Practicing With Concrete Examples

According to Linda Love, writing for the University of Nebraska Medical Center's ConnectED newsletter, the use of concrete examples when learning abstract concepts is another evidence-based strategy that you should use with your students (Love n.d.). This article uses a commonly cited study by Rawson, Thomas, and Jacoby (2015) on "The power of examples." Basically, we all know that keywords and terms (i.e., declarative concepts) are often building blocks for learning higher level concepts within a subject. Also, instructors and students tend to have an overconfidence or expectation that students will internalize these important keywords and definitions just by looking at them once or twice. We now know that is not how memory works for most people. By using concrete, real-life examples, which are highly relevant to the subject matter, we almost always ensure better retention of these concepts.

Implementation strategies are straightforward: Use case studies, images, data and visualizations, and common patterns in class lectures and activities. With our experience of teaching in the environmental field, we have access to a plethora of data sets and human experiences ranging from coastal flooding to wastewater treatment, to air quality measurement and control. Find examples best suited to your subject.

Practicing With Dual Coding

According to Nottingham Trent University (NTU)'s Centre for Academic Development and Quality, dual coding combines visual and verbal elements to convey information in a way that enhances learner retention and overall engagement (Khabarova n.d.). According to NTU, dual coding was developed under the recognition that the human brain processes information into learning more effectively when multiple sensory modalities are engaged simultaneously. It is called dual because the two commonly paired senses are auditory (or verbal) and visual. By stimulating both senses, you form what are known as representational connectedness.

This is another intuitive notion, but now that you know that it has a name and is based on sound evidence, you can try to incorporate or emphasize it into your teaching. For face-to-face learning, NTU offers four strategies:

1. Use whiteboards, PowerPoint tables, charts, graphs, and concept maps to supplement explanations.
2. Draw out diagrams, write keywords, or display images that visually represent the topical content.
3. Create activities that require students to verbally discuss a visual resource.
4. Use props and manipulatives, or even better, have students manipulate objects while receiving verbal instructions.

All of these are common sense examples, but it is easy to settle on just one of these strategies. Make sure to mix things up and do not underestimate the power of having students actually doing tasks and manipulating objects during class time.

The Irony of the Term "Evidence-Based Practice"

For anyone trained in the sciences and applied fields, it is rather ironic to hear reference to "evidence-based practice." As if science should be anything other than based on evidence. Yet education is full of theory-based practices that seemingly waits for the evidence to come in to back them up. However, there is another meaning to it that is in seemingly direct contrast. Theory-based practice is also known as "learning by doing" and refers to active learning in the classroom and laboratory. This is quite different from its broader conceptual meaning as an approach to pedagogy based in theory rather than evidence.

Thankfully, you do not have to worry about this unless you are actually teaching a course in pedagogy to preservice teachers or possibly to nursing students during their practicum coursework. What you can do is to use the best practices that evaluation and assessment have informed us about how to best learn.

Conclusion

If you are a new adjunct, you may find yourself suddenly thrust into an environment where there appear to be all kinds of theories and practices that could have implications for your teaching. So you may have to assess quickly what is real and what is not real; what will help you and what will hinder you. It is very easy to overthink this and get side-tracked.

Myths and jargon abound in education. To help clarify the waters, you can think of learning preferences rather than styles and realize that the jury is still out on some of the major theories. Many learning theories exist. There is a certain practicality to many of them. Assessments help support what contributes to memory and retention, and what boosts critical thinking. Assessment should be formative for your students and for you, as you build your teaching "toolkit" and continually refine and improve your teaching practices.

It makes sense to acknowledge intrinsic motivation and find extrinsic motivator factors that align with the practical benefits if not the pure joy of learning. Learning theories can support your metacognition about teaching and enable you to nurture the metacognition of your students. This benefits their learning and their ability to think about and plan for additional learning. Examine your educational practices. Discuss them with your mentor, CTL, academic department, chair, academic support services, colleagues, and of course your students.

Improving your students' metacognition means contributing to your own metacognition. Good teaching means facilitating "deep learning," which also contributes to metacognition. Think of metacognition as "mindful teaching and learning." Look for tools and processes that support your teaching. Think of yourself as having two professions, that of the field you are training in or currently practicing in, and the field of education—as an adjunct you are a practitioner in education.

Finally, education has entered an era of lifelong and continuous learning. This is what academics need to do to stay up in their professions and in teaching. And it is what students need to do to have good-quality lives. The more you can instill a love of learning in your students, the more likely they are to become lifelong learners.

CHAPTER 7

On Grading Students and Evaluating Instructors

The Interesting Dichotomy of Grading and Being Graded in Academia

In this chapter, we will consider the interesting dichotomy of grading student work and being evaluated both by our students and our peers. We live in an era of metrics: everything is evaluated using some form of numerical scale. These evaluations are not uniform and not always evidence based. But they serve to set bars for student learning and for getting rehired to teach next term. As a grader, you will sometimes feel frustrated by the performance of your class, angst over having to grade so many papers, and guilt that you might be too harsh in doling out Cs and Ds. As a contract employee, you will feel anxiety over your student evaluations and over that end of semester report that your department provides to the dean. Ah, to be a tenured professor and not care about these trivialities (but fear not, you are escaping much more).

Grading Students

Professionals aiming to get into teaching should understand that grades are not the same thing as assessment (Pope 2001). This may seem surprising to the new contingent faculty member, but grades are generally a final documentation of learning, whereas assessment implies a feedback aspect. Indeed, assessment primarily connotes feedback and growth, as well as a fostering of student agency (Lench 2019). Ultimately, we are expected to come up with grades after our assessments. Turning in those grades is usually the final act of the adjunct under the teaching contract.

Your objective should be to establish your principles of fair grading. You want to establish clear, objective, and consistent grading criteria. And you want your students to know why and how you are doing this. The benefits are not only in a reliable assessment of student performance but also in the boosting of your and your students' metacognition about learning. Likely, this still does not make grading easy for you.

Grading is perhaps one of the least popular activities for teachers. But this distaste can be lessened when we view grading as a documentation of formative assessment. As such, it contributes to student learning in addition to documenting it in a manner that students need to make progress in their educational goals. Regardless, we still need to make grading as effective as possible and to take up as little of your time as possible. Online course management systems can help, as can grading rubrics shared with the students and used for practice and for progressive development of proficiency in tests and assignments.

The syllabus is the place for students to encounter your grading criteria and policies. This means you should decide in advance and as much as you can so everyone knows the rules and there are as few "surprises" as possible. It also reduces challenges because the students see at the outset how things are. Yes, there may be some questions and challenges, but many of these are best dealt with at the start. A student who greatly objects to your methods, such as use of multiple-choice tests, is better off knowing at the start so they can decide if they want to continue in the course or drop it and get their money back (most schools have a point at which no refunds are possible). It is not fun to start a course thinking about students who may drop it but treat it as contingency planning; a worst case scenario in which everyone benefits from knowing early.

Most institutions use the ABCDF and 1.0 to 4.0 grading systems we tend to be familiar with from the earliest grades on. A few schools (Antioch for example) use an evaluative narrative rather than a grading system, but the narrative descriptors roughly translate into letter grade equivalents. For example, a student who has "good work" has B-level work and "very good work" is B+. Regardless, instructors have individual discretion within the range prescribed by the institution. An institution might leave it to the instructor to decide if an A is in the 95 to 100 range, or in the 90 to 100, or the range is prescribed, and the instructor has the description to assign a student's performance to a point within the range. Some instructors use their own point system, which then gets translated to a grade range. For example, high-level proficiency demonstrated on all assignments might be assigned 1,400 points, which might be the equivalent of an A. In such a scheme the high-stakes assignment might be 1,000 points, and a low-stakes assignment might be 50 points. Such systems can get rather complex. Whatever you choose to use, explaining the system to the student and the rationale for using it can help with their understanding and acceptance. Ultimately, it is the instructor's choice, but here is a pro tip: keep it as simple as possible.

Many instructors use "proficiency of accomplishment" in grading, which means that all, some, or even none of the students achieve an A. If all students get an A, some view it as meaning the course was "too easy." But it could be argued, if the grading is fair, that preselection of students as capable of achieving, coupled with the able work of the instructor in motivating students, result in the high achievement of all. Some experiential courses, and pass/fail courses are built this way.

Most instructors do not teach pass/fail courses, but perhaps this time it is you that must do so. In that case, be sure to look at what the criteria are. If you are teaching a pass/fail course, it is important to know the competency level for passing. This can become an issue for students who may need to transfer course credit. There may be some default assumption unless otherwise specified. An example of a problem is if the passing level is "D" and the receiving school accepts only C- or higher, then the student loses all credit for that course. The passing level of competency might be able to be specified as B if all students who pass are expected to have "good" proficiency. The benefit of this accrues to students who can thereby rebut a presumption that a pass/fail represents "minimal" competence.

WTF Is DFW?

A term you will hear in assessment and in discussing student success is "DFW," which means "Ds, Fs, and Withdrawals" or grades of D, F, and W. (Sometimes universities include I "incomplete," AU "noncredit-bearing audit," UAU meaning "unsatisfactory audit"—see how confusing academia makes things?) Whatever specific meaning is assigned, a high DFW for your class and your department is not good. DFW rates correlate negatively with retention of students. Institutions try to keep the DFWs below 10 percent of course enrollments. DFWs can be used in faculty evaluations either directly or indirectly as in making decisions about who to rehire. Faculty are expected to maintain certain standards, particularly when the course develops critical thinking, knowledge, skills, and abilities for subsequent courses. But teaching a course in which too many students drop or fail is not good for the higher education academic career prospects of contingent faculty (or untenured professors; tenured professors may be beyond such worries). Schools that track their DFWs, which they must increasingly do to be competitive, will often reach out to instructors of courses that have low DFWs. Intervening teaching techniques that boost student engagement, coupled with increased support of students outside of the course itself have been shown to reduce DFWs (Marwaha et al. 2021).

Norming of Grades

You are hired for your expertise and ability, so go ahead and trust yourself. Yes, you want to be firm and yes you want to be fair. You are in a business where people question things, so you will be thinking about whether you are doing the right thing. You can bet your students are doing that as well.

If you are new to teaching, it will not be long before a student tells you that you are the only one not giving them A's. Certainly, there is a leveling or norming effect as you mesh what your expectations are, what your students can do, and what you can reasonably expect them to do. This can be a particularly troublesome issue if you are teaching one section of the course in which other instructors are teaching and assigning much different grades.

We have handled this issue in our role as senior faculty by sharing with other course faculty examples of student work (usually high quality) with our annotations on it, the student's name removed (however, only use work for which you obtain the student's permission to use). We also put our standards and expectations in the syllabus and on the course website. We ensure that these expectations and other procedures comport with department policies. But not all departments do this kind of reaching out and sharing. You might consult with a faculty mentor, department chair, or other faculty. That said, it is your decision—you are the professional and you know what you are doing, so trust yourself and your students will too.

For reality checks, you may find support and examples in the instructional materials that accompany the textbook you use. Teacher subject area blogs, conferences, and workshops are also sources. Use the CTL at your institution, you will be glad you checked in with them. The formative assessments you give to students will give you perhaps your most useful source of feedback—students themselves. TAs, both undergraduate and graduate, will likely be students with previous experience and insight into reasonable expectations and how they play out.

Navigating Grade Pressures

Adjuncts may feel particularly vulnerable to grade demands from students if they fear not being rehired due to being strict. On the other hand, there is a certain amount of freedom in being there on a specific contract term for a course—you can be honest and move on. Either way, as an instructor you owe it to yourself, your colleagues, and most of all to your students to give honest, fair grades. Leniency in grading hurts faculty and students (O'Grady 2023). Harsh grading as a "tough love" approach should be avoided too, but having high expectations and grading accordingly has been shown to boost student performance

(Mahnken 2023). Experienced teachers find this is particularly true when the assessments are formative (Duprey 2024). Your students will respect you for respecting them by expecting them to perform well and giving them a chance to do so.

Contract Grading

"Contract grading" is one form of standards-based assessment that can reduce anxiety for students by helping them to know and plan for expectations. It reduces the pressure on grades, which can detract from student learning. However, all grading is to a certain extent some form of contract grading in that you are likely to put a description of quantity and quality of work that corresponds to an A, B, C, and so forth. But contract grading is more explicit. Students can review a menu of assessments and select from them to create a contract that demonstrates their learning. This can be done individually or by the class as a group. Contract grading has been shown to reduce stress, boost motivation, and model translatable skills (Strong, Davis and Hawks 2004; Litterio 2018). Some see contract grading as problematic when students have to meet specific performance standards, particularly in STEM fields (where there is a significant amount of additive "vertical" learning), and grades are given for participating ("trying") rather than achieving (Ellwanger 2022). Contract grading does not "give away the store" or degrade standards if done properly. However, as an adjunct, it is best to be careful with contract grading unless you have had significant experience with it and it is supported at your hiring institution.

Addressing Incompletes and Exceptions

Your syllabus should state your policy on giving students incompletes. You may not have the same flexibility and circumstances as the permanent faculty and your policy might accordingly be different from those of others. Whatever you decide, be sure it is compatible with your institution and department. Some institutions have the incomplete automatically revert to an F after one semester. Others let it linger indefinitely. In some cases, an incomplete does not do the student a favor as it becomes a crutch to avoid good time management or because it reverts to a failing grade. For others, it is a fair option that accommodates life events such as changing jobs or an unplanned illness. Keep in mind as an adjunct that you might not be teaching in a subsequent semester, and it might not be feasible for you to be accepting and grading work. On the other hand, perhaps to a certain extent it is a reasonable obligation, depending on the circumstances of your contract and work environment. If so, do you have the means to achieve it? For some adjuncts, access to online grading and registrar grade management systems may end with your contract.

You don't have to figure everything out in advance. But you must look at the university's policies as you develop your own. We recommend keeping your policy simple. If a student gets an incomplete, will the bulk of coursework be done and does the student have a reasonable chance of finishing? If a student gets an incomplete there should be a fixed reasonable length of time to finish the work and a schedule for how and when it gets done. Other faculty and your institution's CTL may be able to help. If the grade automatically reverts to failing, consider giving a grade based on what the student will have earned and perhaps changing it if the missing material is supplied. Otherwise, you might have a student who, if grading on the partial work already done, might have gotten a C but instead gets an unfinished "incomplete" converted automatically to a "fail." You might instead find that you could have given that student the C as a placeholder and file a revised grade of whatever the student earns after finishing the incomplete.

If you do provide remedies for students with incompletes, be sure to use specific language such as "we agree you have X days to turn in this assignment." Provide the start date for this clock. Anticipate the "what ifs" and provide a "contract" for what the student does, what the instructor does, and how grading will occur. If you can, create a written document for this and have the student sign it. Again, if possible, put your policy in the syllabus so the students know upfront. As with most of these gray area policies, try to be kind, fair, and transparent.

Keep a Paper Trail

Keep a record of any "off syllabus" agreements, as it will start you down the slippery slope of individualized exceptions. It is always wise to keep a uniform set of rules for the entire class. However, inevitably you will encounter "the negotiator"—a student who tries their best to bend the rules to their benefit. There are students who have legitimate issues crop up, whether it be falling ill, having to care for a loved one or some other reason. If you do relent and offer an exception, it is extremely important to maintain a record of the renegotiated contract. Otherwise, it can often lead to a difference of opinion on what accommodation was agreed upon. You do not want the student to go to another professor or the department chair or for the emboldened, straight to the academic dean with their complaint. But it is an option for them and if you have a good paper trail, it can protect you as well. The grading system, student advising notes, or other proprietary system used by your institution may also have an opportunity for online documentation of events such as "met with student X on such and such a date and we agreed they would do Y." Similar results could be achieved with a note to the student's adviser or to the academic standards office, or even an email to yourself. If the student does "go above your head" and reports you to the dean, at least you have a shield to protect yourself with.

Rubrics

A rubric is a written document of the criteria the student is expected to use in creating the assignment or performing the assessment, and these criteria are supposed to be the criteria you use in evaluating the assignment or assessment and assigning a grade to it. A rubric is clearly needed especially if it is an unfamiliar form of assessment. You want to know for yourself and the student what constitutes "excellent" work, what is acceptable work, what is unacceptable, and so on. How are these criteria measured? How specific do you want to be? According to the Academy for Teaching and Learning at Baylor University (2024), a rubric can be broad ("holistic") or analytical, or descriptive. It can range from very simple to quite complex. Rubrics are recommended for all assignments and assessments, but it is up to you how much to articulate each rubric and how to present them to the student. Your CTL likely has models and templates—NC State (2024) has an excellent online resource, titled "Rubric Best Practices, Examples, and Templates." They even recommend using ChatGPT to help you create your own! Additionally, plenty of examples and advice can be found online. Try out your rubric with sample work so you see how it serves your objectives and how easy and effective it is for you and the students.

Confidentiality Considerations

A student's performance in the classroom as documented by grades is a sensitive matter that raises confidentiality issues. Recall that FERPA is the Family Educational Rights and Privacy Act. It applies to public and private K-12 and higher education (i.e., everyone) and covers how academia needs to keep student information confidential. Schools will have individual policies to implement FERPA, this will include things such as not posting grades and not releasing information about the students. Once the student is 18, this privacy means even their parents (or spouse) do not get information about their academic performance, regardless of whether or not they are paying tuition, room, and/or board.

You are not violating FERPA to discuss a student's academic performance with their academic adviser or others with a clear need to know in conjunction with the performance of their duties. You do need to take care in preserving confidentiality in materials you may have such as graded papers. They should not be left out for anyone to see. When it comes to writing reference letters, we don't think someone would complain if you said "Jennie got an A in my class," but you are better off avoiding any grade references and say things like "Was an excellent student." Even better, give concrete examples of positive areas. Maybe Johnny did not get all As, but perhaps you can say "always had excellent margins on his papers."

Student rolls often contain personal information, including home address, current address (if living off campus), and often telephone numbers. The only time it is acceptable to use this information is if there is a legitimate concern for the student's personal safety. If you are concerned that a student may be in imminent danger, you can work with the institution's office of students or counseling program and with public safety to try to locate the person.

Evaluating Faculty

Most institutions in the United States and elsewhere require regular teaching observations of all their faculty (Byrne, Brown, and Challen 2010). "Regular" faculty are usually evaluated based on teaching, service, and research, in some specified ratio. These factors do relate and reinforce each other. For example, quality research is positively associated with quality teaching (Cadez, Dimovski, and Zaman 2015). For regular faculty, teaching acts primarily as a negative feedback mechanism, meaning good teaching will not get you promoted or retained, but bad teaching can get you fired (Insider Higher Education 2010). For adjuncts, teaching is what you are there for, so it is everything.

Adjunct faculty are generally evaluated solely on the basis of teaching. Regular part-time faculty (or "temporary full-time") might also have some service requirements that are reflected in their evaluation. Instructors, lecturers, and professors who hold nonresearch appointments will be evaluated based on teaching and service. Tenured and tenure-track faculty are typically evaluated based on teaching, service, and research, often equally divided among all three, or at least expressed that way in governance documents and contracts.

As you might expect, there is often some difference between how a university evaluates faculty and how it says it evaluates faculty. The implications of this for you as an adjunct is to be careful about being lured into service activities that benefit the university but not your teaching. Ironically, you may have to be proactive in getting your teaching evaluated. Many institutions simply do not have the resources to directly observe the adjunct's teaching. This means a significant portion of their evaluation tends to be student-influenced if not student-led. Yet student evaluations can be quite biased (Keenan 2022; more on this in the following). Consequently, anything you can do to get input or evaluation from your chair or other faculty will help you.

Schools abound at collecting data. You will likely have to give some kind of assessment survey to your students to complete where they answer dozens of questions evaluating the course and you. It is a little harder to see how schools use this other than default ranking of course or instructor popularity, but they are supposed to use it to improve instructions and student learning. Course evaluation is a touchy subject in academia (Medina et al. 2019). But as an adjunct, you probably do not want to rock the boat. So see if you can add questions to the course evaluation form that will directly improve your teaching, since most of the questions used will be ranking questions, and not open-ended suggestions for improvement. Unfortunately, the institution's course evaluation form is usually summative; handed out or accessed at the end of the course, precisely when it will do you the least good in adjusting before the semester is over, although you certainly can use it for improving your next course. The formative assessments and evaluations to benefit your current course are most likely to be the ones you come up with on your own.

Another option, if there is not a built-in peer observation, is to ask a colleague to observe your teaching. Or a guest speaker could be a source of feedback to you. If you are able to get a faculty mentor, that would be a good person to observe your teaching through passively sitting in on your class, or as a guest speaker or panelist for student presentations. Someone who comes into your class to view student products or presentations may not directly observe your teaching but can see how you have set things up and how the students interact with you. Such feedback can be valuable. Most institutions will have guidance for peer teacher observations and other aspects of faculty evaluation.

Student Evaluations

Course/instructor evaluations have been used widely in American universities for a century or more (Zabaleta 2007). Typically, a student will receive an opportunity to fill out these evaluations for each class that they complete during a given semester, typically four. For decades, these bubble sheet forms would be handed out during the last couple weeks of class, filled out and collected for further analysis. Now, most evaluations are completed using an online portal during a small window of time at the end of the semester and the number of questions can run from 20 to 50 depending on if an instructor chooses to add additional questions.

Students are highly encouraged but not required to complete these evaluations. However, institutions want evaluations and use a variety of methods to get them. Some institutions delay posting grades or offer incentives. Evaluations are anonymous and contain additional free response spaces for the student to leave personalized commentary. After the semester is completed, faculty are provided end-of-term evaluation reports that can be used as a gauge for how the course went that semester, including how students perceived the professor's teaching style, command of the material, all the way down to how the student felt the workload was in comparison to their other courses.

There are several implications for the use of student-completed evaluations in the higher education setting. Originally, these evaluation instruments were just simple pedagogical tools used for course and instructor improvement for the next time that course was offered. However, they have morphed into much more than they probably should be used for. They have been known to be used in tenure and promotion decisions, in program evaluation, and in student course or instructor choice. For contingent faculty, they have been used to determine whether they receive an invitation to teach the following term or academic year (Beran and Rokosh 2009).

A recent opinion piece by Len Gutkin in *The Chronicle of Higher Education* highlights what many view as significant flaws in their use for anything more than to help instructors self-evaluate (Gutkin 2023). Where do we begin? First, students are not trained in pedagogy and have never actually taught a course. They are evaluating how they feel about the class. They are evaluating *perceived* effectiveness. Also, sample size is important. Because these evaluations are not mandatory and no longer filled out by a physical form in class, we've personally experienced 10 percent compliance especially at the peak of COVID. A sample size of five students or fewer is not enough to offer meaningful information and chances are the ones that bothered to fill out the evaluation hated or loved you and the class. Also, the timing of the evaluations is problematic. End of semester is the worst time to release evaluations. Students are fatigued, stressed out with deadlines, and it's too late to make any changes to the course. Additionally, students can't really gauge the value of what they learned so close to being done with the material. We can cite so many examples of former students complaining about assignments they had to complete, which ended up equipping them with useful skills in the workplace.

One final piece of evidence pointing to the potential flimsiness of using course evaluations in making administrative decisions comes from a medical school study, wherein the instructors handed out chocolate cookies to the class (Hessler et al. 2018). This playful but rigorous study was performed on 118 unsuspecting third-year German medical students who were randomly divided into groups. During an emergency medicine course, half of the group were provided with 500 grams of chocolate cookies to share while the other half, the control group, received nothing. After the course, all the students completed an extensive questionnaire, which asked them to rate the instructor, the course contents, the teaching materials, and to provide a self-assessment. The study authors found that the group that received cookies evaluated their instructors significantly higher than did the control group. In fact, all variables that were evaluated by the students were all higher and statistically significant in the cookie group. It was Germany, so the chocolate was probably delicious, but if such a minor intervention can impact the attitudes of a class that significantly, then it calls into question the validity of using evaluations in administrative decisions.

So, what are the lessons here for you as an adjunct? Well, for one, higher education has not been immune to the prevalence of the use of rating systems in practically every facet of American consumerism. We rate products on Amazon, services on Yelp and Google Reviews, we rate our physicians on Health Grades, there even is a higher ed version called "Rate My Professor." (Warning: only visit that site if you have thick skin.) We have embraced a "ratings culture," and the anonymous nature of these reviews allows for extreme ratings that can be riddled with significant personal bias. So, do your best to provide quality instruction and use the data to help in your self-evaluation, knowing that there will likely be inherent bias in the results (especially if you handed out cookies that semester). Also, feel free to complain about course evals to yourself on your ride home from work.

Peer Evaluation

At many institutions, a peer observation is required for your first assigned course. This means someone from your department sits in on one of your classes and writes a letter or makes notes based on this observation. The difficulty is obvious when you are teaching a night course, and it is a department of only three or four individuals. It simply doesn't get done unless the organization insists on it and works to make it happen. The department chair may ask a faculty member to get in touch with you about attending a class. They might only be there for part of it, particularly if it is a three-hour course that meets only one night a week. Some institutions require formal peer review and assessment, while others merely recommend it.

If your department does not have the resources to do peer reviews for adjunct faculty teaching at night or off campus, you have a few other options. If you have a mentor, consider asking that person to be a guest in your class or to observe it. If you have student projects or presentations, invite a guest to be on a review panel or similar role. Guests can be other faculty, college administrators, or people from your work world. Professional society representatives, government agencies, business connections—all can be potential guest speakers or panelists. They may be in a position to comment on how you handle the class and other factors. If you are using technology with input from the institution's technology center or people, they may be in a position to provide feedback or commentary. Similarly, if you invite a librarian, academic adviser, tutoring center personnel, career services person, or other support office representatives to the class, they will be another observer pool you can dip into. If your course includes civic engagement, you may have a ready source of community partners who could connect with your class.

You should be aware of whether a teaching observation or peer assessment is required so that you can take steps to ensure it happens. You would not want a contract renewal to be held up while someone looks for paperwork that was never filed. If an observation is not required, it is still a good idea to ask for one so that you can add it to your professional portfolio, not to mention that you might also benefit from anything it constructively points out. Further, it may give you an edge over other part-timers competing for your teaching assignment who have not done so. The best place to begin your investigation into teacher observations and peer evaluations is likely to be the department chairperson.

Formal Peer Evaluations and Their Impact

For an adjunct, formal evaluation typically consists of a letter to the personnel file. The letter primarily recapitulates a particular classroom teaching observation or the more general results of observing the adjunct overall. An adjunct should be retaining a teaching portfolio for job application and review with such letters and material relating to their work as an adjunct.

In preparing for formal evaluation (or informal, for that matter), it is a good idea to plan and organize your teaching portfolio. Most institutions that have a CTL will have various guides for faculty. Cornell University (2024) provides a particularly good example of guidance material. According to Cornell, "a teaching portfolio is an opportunity to step back from the immediate demands of teaching to curate representative materials from your teaching journey, reflect, and articulate what you have learned about the ways people learn." You will already have your teaching statement or philosophy if it was required as part of the job application, which it typically is. And you will have added good examples of student products and assignments that reflect your teaching philosophy and how students perform within the context of it.

Cornell suggests that teaching portfolios can be used for meta-cognition or reflection on your growth, aspirations, and values. It can showcase your development and achievements. The portfolio is a formative collection that gets added to and improved over time. Cornell writes, "it allows you to: clarify and refine teaching practices; define your personal teaching style; reflect on your journey as a teacher; clarify your commitment to teaching and learning; focus on the learning process and attainment of course goals; [and] explain to yourself and others the reasons for the ways you teach."

Reflective Practice and Self-Review

Reflective practice is the cycle of teaching, reviewing, and assessing yourself as a teacher, evaluating your assessments, and making changes to your teaching. The goal is to improve your teaching especially in terms of benefiting how students learn effectively. Reflective practice begins with a mindset that you are a continual learner. As such, you desire to improve yourself and seek out opportunities to do so. There are many tools to help you, beginning with the confidence to question yourself in a constructive manner. Ask yourself questions about the effectiveness of your teaching. Be an experimenter. Yes, experimentation can be risky when something does not work, but you can learn from it about best practices. You can collaborate with colleagues to learn what works best for them and whether it is adaptable for you, reviewing their actions and making changes to their practices. If you can, get a colleague to sit in on your class formally as a teacher observer or perhaps in another role such as a guest presenter or evaluator. Keep a notebook of what you do and what you learn from it—essentially "journaling" about your teaching. Take advantage of your improved access to educational research as an adjunct. Use your institution's CTL. If your class is recorded as part of blended or online learning, review the recordings. Or perhaps even record a session for yourself to review.

Teaching Statements: A Self-Evaluation Document

Academic life involves a fair amount of self-reflection and then writing it down for others to review. Recruitment for some contingent faculty positions may require submitting a written teaching statement. Some points to ponder if you are asked to write a statement of your teaching philosophy (and even if you are not): We must know who we are—not just ourselves, but who the members of the department or unit are in terms of orientation to others, strengths, weaknesses, content areas of specialty, preference for teaching styles and values, life/career stages, personality, work preferences, orientation toward students, and other attributes.

Promoting noninvasive aspects of this knowledge and exchange of it might already be codified in your target school or department's official policies and procedures. As an adjunct, you might not have an opportunity to contribute to department governance policies, but you can have your syllabi model your values. For example, you can insert "collaboration" and "communication" as an expectation of the students in your course and accordingly set up means to evaluate them. We should celebrate our strengths so we can build on our capabilities, but we can also work on our weaknesses. Describe your strengths and how they benefit your students' learning. Identify the areas you are working on as a teacher—what do you want to improve on. The reader should see that you are a lifelong learner who continually builds your knowledge, ability and skills in and outside of the classroom.

In preparing your teaching statement or philosophy, be sure to incorporate your views on formative assessment (especially now that you know what it is). Harvard University (2024) suggests that your teaching statement incorporates three major aspects, a "story about the evolution of [your] teaching beliefs and practices," your "performance of disciplinary mastery," and a "window into your understanding of students." Your own institution's CTL will likely have great examples also.

Working With the Department Chair

In most institutions the department chair is responsible for adjuncts, including hiring and evaluation. In some institutions the chair has the authority to exercise this responsibility, while in other institutions the chair is a member of the faculty but not a manager, and the dean has this authority. Commonly, there is a mismatch between authority and responsibility (Dettmar 2022). Ultimately, it is largely the responsibility of the chair, as the person with "boots on the ground" in the subject area or department.

The department chair is a person who usually admittedly values and promotes departmental culture. Most serve as chair as part of being a good university citizen and do not aspire to higher administrative positions (Armstrong and Woloshyn 2017), making them ideal for supporting you in a direct role. When the chair finds out that you value good teaching and are seeking to improve yourself as an adjunct faculty member, they will likely be delighted to support you. Chairs realize the value of good teaching and the difficulty of getting good adjuncts (McGlynn 2022).

Department chairs are typically overworked and stretched to the limit, so they will try to be very efficient in what they do. This might result in them seeming not to have much time for you. But if you reach out, they will see you care about teaching your students, and they will likely make themselves available to you. Much of what the chair can do will be advisory, but the influence of this person cannot be overemphasized. Deans rely on their chairs for input and recommendations about course offerings and hiring adjuncts.

Conclusion

Assessment is a broad brush. We try to figure out what students know, how they know, and what they can do with their knowledge. We try to get students to think about this too. We have to turn in grades, and that certainly is one thing that gets their attention. If we do assessment right, we use it in a formative fashion that encourages student metacognition about their learning. Admittedly, a new adjunct seldom enters the teaching realm thinking about metacognition. Hopefully by now you see it as consciousness and reflection, with the ability to do so intentionally nurtured by the educational experience.

Our assessment tools are what we call assignments and performative demonstrations that we call exams. In helping students prepare assignments and prepare for exams, we give practice opportunities, evaluative guides (rubrics), and ongoing (formative) assessments. We articulate our standards of high expectations for our students and describe the components of how these standards are measured and valued.

We are aware of the grades we give in the content of what occurs in the academy; how our students perform in their studies, but our grades are given in accordance with our assessments and our professional judgment. Thus, our grades have integrity and resist unreasonable norming pressures. We prepare in advance for contingencies such as student illnesses, requests of incompletes, celestial events, and other factors that can affect successful completion of the course by a student. We are aware of success rates (e.g., "DFW" rates) because we and our students benefit from understanding the milieu or context of their educational experience in your course among their greater education pursuits and goals.

Our various assessments in the form of assignments and exams contribute to student learning as well as help measure it. There is informed deliberateness and intentionality in why and how we give assignments and exams. We recognize the need for timely feedback. We pay particular attention to group work and student collaborations, to peer reviews, and to setting up students for success in the course we are teaching.

View your assessment as formative; you want to improve your ability to gather information about student performance and accurately gauge it. You want your assessments to be done in a way that motivates students and fosters student metacognition about their education.

Students are aware that you are assessing them, and they know they will get a chance to evaluate you at the end of the semester. You can assess a student's assessment of you as you progress through the course, if you want. A sort of "how am I doing?" that need not undermine their sense that you actually do know what you are doing.

Conversely, being a good instructor is about being inquisitive and reflective. Your teaching statement should capture your approach to teaching and as a scholar of teaching and learning. Formal and informal assessments and evaluations can help you.

Most institutions include some form of student opinion solicitation as part of faculty evaluation. Student assessments of teaching can be easily overlooked for several reasons. First, students regularly get assessment forms as part of end-of-semester protocols from the institution's assessment office. Students regularly ignore such requests unless they feel strongly or the instructor or institution make an issue out of getting the assessment done.

Pay attention to assessment and evaluation of your work and growth as an instructor, working on these metacognition aspects of your role as an adjunct will benefit you and your students. You will be modeling a good approach for them as potential lifelong learners, and you will gain tools for your teaching, as well as a greater sense of your place in academia,

Your department chair will appreciate your involvement and, along with your institution's CTL, provide resources for your growth (professional development), knowing that will make you into an even better adjunct. Document your development with a portfolio. Many CTLs run workshops on creating and updating a portfolio.

Adjuncts are reliant on good student evaluations to continue to receive a contract. Higher level contingents and tenure-track professors are not. However, all faculty should care and be aware of their strengths and their areas to work on, including how they are perceived by students. Faculty should know that student evaluations are generally better if the professor is nice (respectful), dresses well, and is attractive. It is inevitable that professors get compared to each other based on the student evaluations (regardless of the number of responses). In fact, assessment offices typically report department faculty averages. These can be big factors in peer reviews and in retention decisions. Unsigned comments don't have to be used (and their use might even be prohibited), but unsigned numerical responses have to be used. Further, not everyone gets to see the evaluations. At some public institutions, the department chair and others in the department do not get to see the contingents' (or other faculty's) evaluations; only the dean does. This should be rather shocking news to most contingents who are used to the logic of the business world.

Student assessment of faculty is a regular end of semester ritual, but many students choose not to participate unless they feel strongly one way or another about the instructor or the course. Thus, there are certainly some issues in using these statistics. Most faculty union contracts do not allow unsigned student comments to count. However, unsigned numerical evaluations of various teaching categories (e.g., "how well does the professor know the subject matter?") feed into summary numbers that inevitably rank faculty against "average" numerical standards. Further, unsigned evaluations enable trolling and other inappropriate student communication (Fowler 2019).

Tenure-track and other full-time faculty will have a peer committee that contributes periodic assessments and evaluations to the dean. The peer committee typically does periodic teaching observations. But part-timers and adjuncts typically do not have peer committees, so they may lack that input. As an adjunct, you might have a requirement to be observed. Some academic units require contingent faculty to be observed at least once in the first semester of employment. If there is no requirement for such, it is still an excellent idea to request an observation. This will do two things. It will show you care, and it will provide some feedback that may be helpful in your teaching (and in getting hired for additional semesters). Don't be surprised though, especially if you are teaching at night or off-campus, that the department might not spare someone to do a teacher observation.

CHAPTER 8

Frequently Asked Questions (FAQ)

Here we try to address some questions that you may already have in mind or perhaps we can anticipate some questions that you might like to have in mind. We also include some questions that might have already been addressed in our other chapters, but here we can provide a more succinct quick reference summary. Anyway, here is a chance for us to play catchup on some things that may be helpful to professionals trying to "hack it" in academia.

1. *What qualifications do I need to become an adjunct professor at a community college or university?*

The hiring institution will specifically address this in the position advertisement. Except under unusual circumstances you can expect at least a baccalaureate for the two-year school and at least a master's for the four-year and higher institution. It helps if you have had teaching experience of any sort, formal and informal. If you want to start building your teaching experience, consider volunteering to guest in a course so you get some exposure to being in the front of a classroom. If you have had K-12 teaching experience you may find that is recognized and valued, particularly at two-year schools and for freshman courses at four-year institutions. Professional licensure also gives you an advantage in teaching courses for departments such as nursing and engineering.

2. *How do I find adjunct teaching positions in my field?*

There are lots of places to check for academic jobs. Colleges and universities will post jobs under HR and Employment on their respective websites. A simple web-based search using the school's name and "employment" will almost always provide you with a link to their most recent academic job postings. Additionally, colleges (especially public institutions) often have notification requirements that cause jobs to be listed in local newspapers—digital and print where you can still find them.

There are many higher education and job recruiting websites that also have relevant job postings including higheredjobs.com, jobs.chronicle.com, indeed.com, ziprecruiter.com, and linkedin.com, to name a few. Professional societies and subject-based listervs are also good places to search for positions.

Even if you are not ready to apply for a position, you can begin tracking the local college websites of departments that most pertain to your potential teaching areas of expertise. This will help you gain familiarity with the academic department in terms of its mission, students, faculty, and course offerings. It might also lead to speaking engagements and other means of introducing yourself to potential hiring situations and getting yourself known to the institution.

3. *What documents and information should I prepare for my job application?*

In general, universities and colleges may require your educational and professional background, your criminal background, and any relevant licenses and certifications. Some schools also require official university transcripts. In addition to legal and personal identification documents, you will need a resume, or perhaps a CV. You will probably need a personal teaching statement. Bring letters of reference or lists of reference providers, and letters of teaching observation if you have them. You might also consider developing and having at hand a portfolio of teaching with sample assignments, student projects, and other teaching support materials.

4. *What can I expect during the interview process for an adjunct position?*

Most places will have you first be cleared for an interview by the HR office or department. You will probably meet with the lead hiring person, often the department chair, and maybe one to three others, usually faculty in the department. When you have your interview, be sure to bring the documents you may have already supplied online, particularly a resume and teaching statement. Be able to articulate why you want to teach and what you will bring to the position.

5. *How are courses assigned to adjunct faculty? Can I choose what I teach?*

Typically, the department or curriculum chair makes the teaching schedule for the upcoming academic year well in advance, probably the year before. Most departments are expected to have a relatively regular schedule so that students can complete graduation requirements within four years, so most degree-related courses run on a predictable schedule.

Usually, the senior faculty in a department get top preference for what they want to teach, and when they teach. The adjuncts are more likely to be put into less preferred slots and will likely teach an introductory course or laboratory section. If a regular faculty member is on leave or sabbatical and teaches a specialized course that other regular faculty are unable to teach, an adjunct in that specialization may be hired to teach that course.

Also, a good department chair wants to recruit good candidates and realizes that they may have limited teaching availability, especially if they already have full-time jobs. Thus, many courses taught by part-time contingent faculty might only meet once or twice a week in the late afternoons or evenings. There may be some ability to negotiate if the time slot is not already fixed, but once the course is posted the registrar is reluctant to make changes since all the enrolled students will have to be notified and some might have conflicts.

6. *What is the typical pay for an adjunct instructor, and how is it determined?*

According to a recent survey, per course pay in the United States ranges from $2,000 to $7,000 with 53 percent of respondents stating that they make less than $3,500 per course (Flaherty 2020). The range is affected by the total number of credit hours the course requires as well as the major (engineering, computer science, and business often command higher pay). More than 50 percent of adjuncts say pay should be $5,000 per course, because of all the "off-hour" work that is done to realistically run a class. It is clear that at this level of pay, universities and colleges use the adjunct teaching position as a tool to keep personnel costs as low as possible. As we said earlier in the book, if you are coming in as a working professional to teach one class, make it about the experience and not the pay. The rewards tend to be nonmonetary, which is easier to swallow when you already have full time employment or a pension to draw from.

7. *Can I negotiate my contract or terms of employment as an adjunct?*

Most part-time lecturer salaries are set and standardized at the university level, especially at public institutions. One- or two-year fixed-length research positions also tend to be set. You can expect that there is very little room to negotiate on the compensation, but there is always some wiggle room. The power to negotiate mostly depends on the rigidity of the institution and the market value of new graduates in the subject area you teach.

Many academic institutions, particularly public ones, have only very limited flexibility in salary offers. The salary range will have been cleared through HR after a lengthy process. Offering a salary for a part-time lecturer that is proportionately higher than what many full-time people of higher academic rank make, would cause significant labor issues and unrest among the current employees. Also, the institution is trying to get as much as they can for as little as they can.

But let us face it: if you have the qualifications to teach at a top 20 business school with a book on the *New York Times* best seller list, you are more likely to have negotiating power. Also, if your contract sets specific job duties but your department expects you to attend meetings and/or university events, you may decline or seek additional compensation for any time you work that does not involve instruction and course management, as per the contract.

8. *What kind of orientation or onboarding should I expect as a new adjunct?*

Academia has gradually become more professional about onboarding university hires, including part-time faculty. It used to be that a department chair or dean would just call a potential new adjunct and ask if they wanted to teach (and perhaps it still is at a few private institutions). Now it is common for HR to handle all aspects of the process. Most institutions use software packages and management systems to do this. You will likely be directed to web-based training via your initial HR email introduction, which will only be accessible after obtaining an official .edu email address. If such is your case, probably the academic chair or administrative assistant will give you a tour and an individualized introduction of some sort. Certainly, connect with the institution's teaching center. Finally, you will be impressed with what your own students can tell you if you just ask them.

9. *What are some things I need to know before I start teaching?*

This is related to Question 8. If there is an orientation/onboarding event, try to attend it even though you are not likely to get any economic compensation for doing so. If the event includes a folder packet, it is a very good sign if it contains the following items. If you do not receive a physical onboarding session, keep these as mental notes or points to ask someone, preferably before your first class:

- Verification of when you are "in the system."
- Form I-9 and other identity documents for HR.
- Where/when to park (parking pass/tag, map, policy).
- Where to get an ID card.
- Classroom, building security and access (lab/office key), IT, and custodial services.
- Academic department support services.
- Advice on teaching, CTL information.
- How to put items on reserve/library borrowing privileges.
- Classroom audio/visual support and other technology support.

- Course discounts, gym, and academic privileges.
- HR information, academic department locations, and contacts.
- Textbook ordering support. (Hint: Also ask how to get desk copies and instructor copies.)
- Classroom supply needs (Chalk? Dry erase markers?).
- Photocopier location, access code, and office supplies/services.
- Online course management or LMS tools training.
- Additional onboarding training (for ADA compliance, research compliance, HR).
- Student services locations, emails, and phone numbers.
- Safely getting across campus at night, lockdown procedures, campus closures, notifications, class disruptions, and student injury.

10. *Will I have access to institutional resources such as libraries, labs, or office space?*

Contingent faculty typically have the same rights to use the library, technical services, computing spaces, and other course delivery related services as do regular full-time faculty. The important thing is to get your identification card and university email address as soon as you can, which will mean you are "in the system." Additionally, the department should have some shared office space designated for part-timers. But many two-year institutions will not, and the adjunct just hopes there is time before or after class in the classroom for office hours.

11. *What financial support does the institution provide for course preparation and delivery?*

This seldom exists and/or is not well advertised at most places. Some institutions will provide a stipend or compensation for new course development for part-time and full-time faculty. But not for a course that has been taught before unless it is being significantly revamped and converted to online or some other dramatic change in delivery or format. For those of us coming in to teach a regular course, assume nothing for preparation of it other than access to the institution's support services.

You can expect there to be a CTL that will have useful resources, and some kind of technical support or online training support services. Virtually all institutions offer an LMS for course delivery, which will have training materials. You want to make sure you are brought onboard and into the system as soon as possible so you can have access for these.

12. Are there opportunities for professional development as an adjunct?

Your institution will likely have offerings through its CTL and other support service resources. Adjuncts generally have opportunities similar to regular faculty for those offerings and services because it is all about supporting teaching faculty. Professional societies also often have an educational section, and training or conference opportunities. You may have rights and opportunities as a member of a union for part-time faculty.

13. How do I ensure that I'm included in important communications and decisions in the department?

We are tempted to say that you are likely not missing much by not attending department meetings and that if you do show up at them you will find the other faculty looking at you curiously. However, yes, attending faculty meetings is one way to keep up with what is up. You are unlikely to have time for this, and you really should not have to attend them. It is the chair's responsibility, often delegated to the administrative assistant, to keep you informed of department business pertinent to your course or that could potentially affect your students. There may be a department or university listserv you might want to sign on to. Official college announcements to faculty will probably go to you via your university email because, even as an adjunct, you are a member of the faculty.

14. What happens if my class gets canceled due to low enrollment?

Usually, this is just a risk we all take. It tends not to happen too much because an adjunct is usually brought in to handle a problem—that of a course that needs to be taught or students that need to learn, so that means it is unusual for the course not to run. But not all planning can be perfect. Canceled courses happen, particularly when it is the last in a series of multiple sections offered. The institution may feel a sense of obligation to have you back at the next opportunity.

15. *What if I need to miss a class due to illness or emergency? What is the protocol?*

Your institution will likely have a policy for this, as might your academic department, so be sure to check with the contract, then your chair, or even the administrative assistant. Accredited schools expect a certain number of contact hours per credit hour, which can be jeopardized by canceling classes. Instead, consider having the students meet independently to work on a class assignment during class time, or have a colleague cover class. If you notify your department chair in advance, they may be able to help you come up with the best solution. Sometimes, there is no alternative but to have an email sent out to students and a sign posted on the door when class simply cannot be held.

If it is a tornado or snowstorm or similar event, the school will have a policy and a procedure for students to find out if all classes are canceled or if class is "optional." Some institutions have makeup policies or shift to remote learning under certain conditions. You certainly do not want to risk deadly harm to get to class nor do you want your students to do so.

16. *What are the expectations for grading and providing student feedback?*

Students expect their work to be graded promptly and likely will be inquiring by the next day and complaining after a week. Pedagogically, feedback is best for learning when most immediate. This gives you the important opportunity to correct misconceptions at the outset. Further, students' final scores tend to be higher than students who receive delayed feedback (Attali and Powers 2009). Pro tip: Plan your assignments so that you do not have mountains of grades. Reviewing drafts for projects and presentations can mean less work for you during grading time. Having grading rubrics should help reduce the load as well.

As a global concern, you will be given a timeline for the course completion and turning in of final grades, and probably reminders from the registrar's office. Prompt turning in of final grades will help your students get their financial aid in time to choose classes for the next semester. And it will reduce stress on your department chair. Your chair can advise you on department and institution protocols.

17. *How should I manage office hours if I don't have a permanent office on campus?*

Faculty should offer regular office hours (often called "student hours") and "hours by arrangement." This is routinely stipulated in the teaching contract. You can consider hosting virtual hours online, but some institutions require a physical presence. Another option is to hold hours before or after your class meeting time. Check if there is another class scheduled to meet in your assigned room before or after. Some adjuncts use the academic department's main office to hold student hours while others use the library, student commons, or other institutional public space. It is advisable to use a room with a door in case some verbal privacy is required but preferably one that has glass walls.

18. *What is an LMS and why is it important in modern education?*

If you work in the world of large corporations, you likely already use an LMS for training, collaborations, and continuous education. In academia, the LMS is used to manage a course. Students submit assignments, view lectures, access course materials, communicate and collaborate with other students, track grading, and many other things. Traditional-aged students will almost certainly have used an LMS unless they were home-schooled. Older students may be less likely to have encountered them. The LMS will have practice areas ("sandboxes") for students and instructors to help get used to what an LMS can do. In most cases, the students will not be able to access the LMS for your specific course until you make it "live" and grant them access.

An LMS is particularly useful for hybrid ("blended") and online courses. They are a great way to track turned-in assignments. You will be able to mark papers with a virtual pen just like you would with physical copies, should you choose to, and track revisions and drafts. When we first started teaching, we had to build MS Excel Workbooks to calculate grades (yes, that is showing our ages) but the LMS will do that for you. If you are worried about access or system crashing, you might also keep a physical copy of your gradebook, but you will come to appreciate the convenience of the LMS.

You will be expected to at least post a syllabus on the course LMS and probably also to be using it for grades, communication, assignments, and such. It is advisable to take time to learn about and practice with the LMS before the semester starts.

One final thing to be aware of is that you might use the LMS gradebook section to compute, track, and report grades for your course, but this will probably not automatically connect to the Registrar. This means that when you enter your final grades into the LMS, you may need to *also* enter those grades into the registrar's system.

19. *What are my responsibilities regarding academic integrity and student plagiarism?*

Many colleges and universities require students to abide by an academic integrity statement. Sometimes these statements require a student signature and if suspected of being violated, students will be required to go through a procedural review. However, you must witness the violation or have sufficient firsthand evidence to initiate a violation report. It is not enough for a third party to report a violation to you.

Additionally, most institutions require or expect this to be addressed in the syllabus and will have language you can use. The institution will probably have an online service to check for plagiarism, likely integrated into the LMS used by your institution. Universities are still experimenting with generative AI checkers, and guidance will continue to evolve in this area.

Our best advice to offer on this is if a first violation seems accidental, provide a warning. If it is repeated or blatant, then gather your evidence and follow the university procedure for reporting. Keep in mind that you owe it to the other students, yourself, and the institution to promote student integrity and to address plagiarism.

20. *How can I help students access and utilize library resources effectively?*

Librarians are usually quite happy to visit a class or provide a personal orientation to you. Typically, libraries provide computer access and guidance to working with online resources. Your department may have a librarian assigned to provide services to it, which may include reference materials and search guides specifically for your course. Some students may benefit from a reminder to use the library and find out just how helpful the staff can be. Dovetailing with Question 19, librarians are also excellent resources for students on what constitutes plagiarism and can be very helpful with additional support in that area.

21. *How do I deal with challenging student behaviors or conflicts in the classroom?*

A lot can be done by simply being a good instructor. But sometimes problems are inevitable. Most situations can be handled with a quiet word to the student. Try to do so in a manner that causes the least embarrassment to the student. You might reach out to the student's professional or academic adviser, or support services such as the office of disabilities if the student is registered with them. Some institutions offer training in dispute resolution, usually for among peers but this may also be helpful in dealing with students. The Dean of Students will likely be a good resource, but first you might want to start with advice from your department chair or mentor if you are assigned one. Remember to keep track of (document) what you say and do.

There is a point at which behavior issues cross over from being troublesome or even annoying into being disruptive. The institution will have a policy for dealing with disruptive students. Allowing disruption interferes with the learning of other students and must be handled promptly. In extreme conditions, you may need to call campus security. For anything less than that, contacting the Dean of Students office and/or a student conduct board of some sort should suffice.

22. *How can I effectively manage and accommodate a diverse classroom with varying student needs?*

Research ahead of time so you know if you have any special-needs students or other circumstances. You will typically receive a letter from the student disabilities office but that will only happen if a student self-reports and sometimes that letter may not arrive until a few weeks into the semester. You may find students who you feel (or they feel) need accommodations but have not visited the institution's student support offices to address this. You need to promptly refer such students, copying their academic or professional adviser, as soon as you can so they can get the support they need. There is a risk in just coming up with accommodations on your own in that other students may perceive favoritism on your part and find it unfair.

Further, the sooner such issues are addressed by the proper support personnel the sooner the student gets what they need, and improves their chances for success in your course and higher education in general. But also know that accommodations are requests, not orders. If the accommodation greatly impacts your ability to deliver the course in a way that is detrimental to the class, you may be unable to provide for that accommodation. If you cannot find an alternative solution, it is best to bring the chair and student services into the conversation to see what if anything can be done.

Beyond providing for special-needs accommodations, plan out your course with projects and "action steps" that support your course objectives, which in turn lead to achieving your overall course goal. If you promote active learning, student metacognition, and frequent low-stakes assessments, you should tune in quickly on student ability and performance, even with no evidence of demonstrated special needs. This will enable you to make mid-course adjustments and corrections that promote student learning. Also take advantage of insights from the CTL, the department chair, and other faculty. Know the student support services and teaching support services available on campus.

23. *What are the key policies I need to be aware of regarding FERPA and student privacy?*

As discussed in the book, FERPA is the Family Educational Rights and Privacy Act. It applies to all academic institutions and covers how academia needs to keep student information confidential. Once a student reaches 18 years of age, this privacy means even their parents do not get information about their academic performance, regardless of whether or not they are paying tuition, room, and/or board.

Student rolls often contain personal information, including home address, current address (if living off campus) and often telephone numbers. The only time it is acceptable to use this information without advanced permission is if there is a legitimate concern for the student's personal safety. If you are concerned that a student may be in imminent danger, you should work with the University's counseling program and with public safety to try to locate the person. When in doubt, check with the Registrar's office or your department chair. Academic institutions must pay close attention to FERPA and as a faculty member you represent the institution to your students and the public.

24. *What are some common pitfalls new adjuncts face and how can I avoid them?*

Adjuncts who fail to know their students are at risk for getting into trouble with their teaching. When in doubt about an issue with a student or a student's learning, make it a point to talk to the student. Try not to be the person who rushes in, teaches their class, then rushes out. Know what else your students are doing and what their workloads are.

Finding the balance of what is the right workload to assign students and how to evaluate them are two of the most common problems new faculty face. Some first instructors have a hard time finding the norm for assessments and expectations. This may be influenced by your own background. People who have freshly arrived from Carnegie 1 research (i.e., R1) institutions might find things are quite different at a small satellite state college.

Your role as professor includes being the bridge between the student and the reading. Much of the learning is put on the student to do outside of class. Consider how to encourage students to do this efficiently. They should know the expectations for time spent outside of class. They should know the difference between reactive studying and strategic studying, and how to use both. Reactive studying is cramming before a test (test-activated studying). Strategic studying is studying 15 to 20 minutes a day to retain the information long term, so you don't have to cram the day before the exam.

Another problem is figuring out what to put in the syllabus—what is too little and what is too much. Your syllabus should inform the students of the work assignments, the assessments, the due dates, and the policies for submittals. For example, you do not want to be printing out student term papers for them because you are an adjunct with limited time and access to a printer other than your own. You probably do not even have your own office at the college. So if you want things submitted online say so, and in what format. LMSs such as Blackboard and D2L Brightspace take care of this. But learning these systems can be a course in its own right, something you may not have time for. Maybe you already learned how to use one for your own college work, but the odds are your new institution will use a different one. Again, something to think about.

Finally, an instructor almost always is received better by students if they take the time to know and understand them for individual and group dynamics. To do so, consider asking the following questions and work to answer them as soon as possible:

- How many students are there? When are the last add and drop dates for enrollment?
- Where do I find a class list, student background, and student photos?
- Who is the primary target for this course—whose needs are most important? (This target audience need not be the largest number of students in the course.)
- Will they be mostly commuters or residential?

- What other constraints or factors challenge them?
- What is their primary motivation for taking this course?
- What percentage of them has already taken a course in this field?
- What percentage of them will likely take another course in this field?
- How good are their math, computer, critical thinking, and writing skills?
- How many have jobs, families, and other nontraditional characteristics?
- Who has computing access at home or outside the university?
- Who needs accommodations? What resources can help them? Ex.: Peer tutors, Learning Center, Dean of Students, Disability Services Office, Course Teaching Assistants, Writing Assistants, Career Services, Housing Services, Financial Aid, Registrar, Reference Librarians?
- How do I connect with each student's academic/faculty adviser?
- What additional training and support do I need to best serve these students?

25. *What strategies can I use to engage students from the beginning of the semester?*

How you start your class will constitute your first impression and you know how lasting those are. Jump right in with activities that supplement or replace a lecture. Carefully plan but allow some flexibility from spontaneity and "reading the room" such as, for example, determining that students need to get up and move around, or discuss a particular burning topic.

For your long-term strategy, consider the benefits of teaching at three levels simultaneously: (1) what all students need to be successful in the class, (2) what the exceptional students need to be challenged, and (3) what you need to do to keep things alert and entertaining to yourself and any students that care to follow. Yes, that means having a sense of humor and keeping things lively. Whatever you do, treat the students as equals to you and among themselves. Respecting them does mean you can assume that they are prepared for the course and have done the readings, but you also have to consider that life happens, and things can intervene despite the student's best intentions. Also, never teach "down" to them. One of the worst things a professor can do is teach to the lowest performing student only. Teaching at a higher level can help pull students into learning at that level. And it helps keep the instructor alert.

26. *How do I handle large class sizes and maintain effective student engagement?*

Plan your class in advance so you can see how best to use active learning in the classroom. Anticipate the class size and be sure the physical space will let you do the activities you want to do. Visit the classroom in advance of your course and get access to additional information other than the student's name and major.

If your course has been run before, seek input from whoever has already taught it. Your department chair will be able to give you a sense of the students and what sorts of things might work best with them. Then get to know the students yourself. Ask for and use student names by talking to them. Use worksheets and walk around the classroom to help you learn the students by seeing their names on the worksheets and interacting with them.

Large class sizes can be a challenge to people who want to do something other than just lecture. There are lots of tools you can use, ranging from TAs (if you are fortunate enough to have one assigned to your class), to small group activities, to immediate feedback assessment tools with the use of technology. Even if you do not have good technology, you can use simple tools such as colored index cards for students to "vote" on the answers to a question posed to the class.

27. *What should I do if I realize mid-semester that my teaching approach isn't working as well as I had hoped?*

Good for you for recognizing this and presumably soliciting and assessing student feedback. Here is where you can immediately seek advice from your department chair, peers, and CTL. You will gain respect for trying to improve things right away rather than wait for the next semester. Students appreciate a candid approach in the interest of improving their learning.

28. *How much is too much work?*

Academic burden is the excessive load placed on students. It includes assigning lots of homework, enforcing rigid rules with punitive consequences, and applying unrealistic grading standards. The result creates a burdensome learning environment for students, but not necessarily an effective one. Our experience has been that instructors who create that type of learning environment often do so to obscure their inability to teach the course content or to teach in general. Thus, the impression is students do poorly not because the instructor was bad, but because the instructor is "tough."

Academic rigor on the other hand means having standards. That is good. Standards exist in the workforce and most people expect high standards to be placed on services and products they purchase in the real world. The same should apply to learning an important subject. Grades, despite their negative connotations, can help you regulate the standard for your class. Provide opportunities for earning points early on through graded homework, small papers, in-class quizzes, and the like. You will quickly be able to gauge what you would consider a high but realistic bar. Rubrics also go a long way in setting appropriate standards. If you have trouble meeting your own rubric expectations, then you know you might be burdening more than providing rigor.

Finally, you can also answer this question analytically. If the school is on the credits semester system, 12 credits is considered to be full time (assuming one regular course is 3 credits), but 15 credits is actually needed to complete a bachelor's degree of 120 credits in 4 years. The 12 credits represent approximately 40 hours per week of work between class time (assume a little over an hour in the classroom and 2.5 to 3 hours of homework per credit hour). These ratios will help you in figuring what time you can reasonably expect students to spend on assignments. A student taking 15 credits per semester should be logging about 50 hours per week of work. Of course, many students will spend 60 or more hours per week on schoolwork, but others simply cannot, particularly in today's era where "nontraditional" students with associated life responsibilities are as much the norm as "traditional" students. The college expectation of study time is more than twice the time expected in high school, but probably much less than many professors would like it to be.

29. Where can I find examples and templates of assignments, classroom activities, and rubrics?

There are two places you should always look to find examples and templates to help ease your transition into teaching a new course. The first is your department. Chances are that you are not creating a class from scratch. Ask the department chair to put you in contact with whoever last taught the class and ask for their notes, assignments, rubrics, and classroom activities. You may not end up using any of them; however, they will almost certainly help frame how to teach the class. The second place to look is your CTL or the various other CTLs that exist at most other universities.

30. What if I am teaching one section (or more) of multiple section offerings in the department?

If you are teaching courses with multiple class sections, find out who the other instructors are and consider meeting with them to coordinate various aspects of the course, including student performance expectations. A good academic department will likely be offering opportunities and guidance for this. If you are feeling lucky and decide to teach two sections of the same course in the same semester, your preparation essentially reduces in half, especially if you can keep the same pace in each section. You may have different classroom management concerns however, since all classes have their own "personality."

31. What should I do if a student challenges their grade on a paper or exam?

You are human and will likely screw up on the grading of a question on an assignment or exam. So you may be inclined to accept a student's appeal of a grade. Give the student the benefit of the doubt; however, it is very likely you graded another question softly or marked another question correct when it was in fact incorrect. Also be mindful of the student who says you marked their exam answer incorrect, but a classmate's equivalent response was marked correct. All these variables become difficult to manage and create a chaotic environment for students and instructors.

We suggest that if you accept a student appeal, advise the student that you will regrade the entire exam and that if you find errors in grading elsewhere, the student may end up with a lower grade than they started with. You probably want some kind of cutoff time for a student to appeal so that you are not always in grading limbo and can move on to the next assignment.

Not that it will ever happen (ahem), but if you made a mistake in grading, own it and fix it as soon as you find out. Most students will appreciate the fact that you are only human and therefore more likely to tolerate errors on their part too. That said, be aware of the grade appeal process and how it works, including how appeals can go up the chain of command to a dean. Some students may aim for the dean or higher, not realizing that the chain of command starts lower. In such cases, do not worry, it will eventually come back down to where it needs to start.

32. *What should I realistically expect from my students?*

We will answer this last question with some observations made by a colleague of ours who works at a different institution. When it comes to realistic expectations from students going to college in the 2020s, he observes:

- Students rarely read the book, if they buy it to begin with (and of course even more rarely if they don't buy it).
- Students rarely take notes because they're expecting the notes to be posted online, and a study guide provided for tests.
- Students are often smart and motivated but easily discouraged/obstructed in their efforts—they will often stop at the first roadblock rather than problem-solve a solution.

- Students often view instructors as a mix of teacher and customer service representative.

Upon reading this, we chuckled because we have made similar observations and made a whole podcast show to comment on many of these same points. (Caveat: there are always outliers—some special students will truly blow you away by their intelligence, effort, and charisma.) We also agree with a clarifying statement our colleague provided after making these observations. "These are not generational criticisms; rather, it is the ongoing evolution of education and learning environments. Students expect learning to be entertaining, relevant, and dynamic. Embrace it and find the many strengths that students bring, or else it's easy to get burned out."

References

AAUP. 2023. "Contingent Faculty Positions." *AAUP Resources*. Accessed November 30, 2023. www.aaup.org/issues/contingency.

Academic Impressions. 2012. "Supporting Adjunct Faculty: An Investment in Your Instructors, an Investment in Your Students." Accessed June 7, 2024. www.academicimpressions.com/supporting-adjunct-faculty-an-investment-in-your-instructors-an-investment-in-your-students/.

Academy for Teaching and Learning at Baylor University. 2024. "Grading Rubrics." Accessed September 27, 2024. https://atl.web.baylor.edu/teaching-guides/assessing-student-learning-and-teaching/grading-rubrics.

Adam, L. 2016. "Student Perspectives on Plagiarism." In *Handbook of Academic Integrity*, edited by T. Bretag, 519–535. Springer, Singapore.

Allan, K. 2012. "5 Myths About Independent Scholars." *Kathryn Allan's Blog*, October 2. Academic Editing Canada. Accessed October 22, 2023. www.academiceditingcanada.ca/blog/item/99-indy-scholar-myths.

Akresh-Gonzales, J. 2019. "Spaced Repetition: The Most Effective Way to Learn." *NEJM Group Education*, May 17.

Akst, Jef. 2012. "So You Want to Write a Book." *The Scientist*, October 1. Accessed November 20, 2023. www.the-scientist.com/careers/so-you-want-to-write-a-book-40420.

Armstrong, D.E., and V.E. Woloshyn. 2017. "Exploring the Tensions and Ambiguities of University Department Chairs." *Canadian Journal of Higher Education* 47 (1): 97–113.

Attali, Y. and D. Powers. March 2009. "Immediate Feedback and Opportunity to Revise Answers to Open-Ended Questions." *Educational and Psychological Measurement* 70 (1): 22–35.

Bain, K. 2004. *What the Best College Teachers Do*. Cambridge: Harvard University Press.

Beall, J. 2017. "What I Learned From Predatory Publishers." *Biochemia Medica* 27 (2): 273–279. https://doi.org/10.11613/BM.2017.029.

Benjamin, E. 2017. "Why 'Fail Fast, Fail Cheap' Is Stupid." *Linked in*, January 23. www.linkedin.com/pulse/why-fail-fast-cheap-stupid-eyal-benjamin.

Beran, T.N. and J.L. Rokosh. 2009. "Instructors' Perspectives on the Utility of Student Ratings of Instruction." *Instr Sci* 37: 171–184. https://doi.org/10.1007/s11251-007-9045-2.

Berke, C. 2023. "The Realities of Working as a College Adjunct Professor." *EdSurge*. February 9. http://dsurge.com/news/2023-02-09-the-realities-of-working-as-a-college-adjunct-professor.

Bollé, L. 2021. "SMART, SMARTER, or SMARTEST: What Kind of Goals Would You Like to Achieve?" *ACB (American Council of the Blind)*. www.acb. org/smart-smarter-or-smartest-what-kind-goals-would-you-achieve.

Boss, G.J., C.J. Porter, T.J. Davis, and C.M. Moore. March 9, 2021. "Who Cares? Black Women as Contingent Faculty and the Leadership Imperative of Labor Justice." *Journal of African American Women and Girls in Education* 1 (1). doi: 10.21423/jaawge-v1i1a19.

Bowen, J.A. 2012. *Teaching Naked: How Moving Technology Out of Your College Classroom Will Improve Student Learning*. San Francisco: Jossey-Bass.

Boyer, E.L. 1997. *Scholarship Reconsidered: Priorities of the Professoriate*. San Francisco: Jossey-Bass.

Boyle, P. 2022. "Why Do So Many Americans Distrust Science?" *AAMCNEWS*, May 4. www.aamc.org/news/why-do-so-many-americans-distrust-science.

Brame, C. 2016. "Active learning." Vanderbilt University Center for Teaching. Accessed October 3, 2024. https://cft.vanderbilt.edu/active-learning/.

Brown, A., and A.N. Kaminske. 2018. *Teaching and Learning Myths–Debunked. A Guide for Teachers*. New York, NY: Routledge.

Bunce, L., A. Baird., and S. Jones. January 14, 2016. "The Student-as-Consumer Approach in Higher Education and Its Effect on Academic Performance." *Studies in Higher Education* 42 (11): 1958–1978.

Burgstahler, S.E., and R.C. Cory, eds. 2008. *Universal Design in Higher Education: From Principles to Practice*. Cambridge: Harvard Education Press.

Burgstahler, S.E., ed. 2013. "Universal Design in Higher Education: Promising Practices. Seattle." *DO-IT, University of Washington*. www.uw.edu/doit/UDHE-promisingpractices/preface.html.

Burnsed, B. 2010. "Degrees Are Great But Internships Make a Difference." *US News and World Report*, April 15. www.usnews.com/education/articles/2010/04/15/when-a-degree-isnt-enough.

Byrne, J., H. Brown., and D. Challen. 2010. "Peer Development as an Alternative to Peer Observation: A Tool to Enhance Professional Development." *International Journal for Academic Development* 15 (3): 215–228.

Cadez, S., V. Dimovski., and M.Z. Groff. 2015. "Research, Teaching and Performance Evaluation in Academia: The Salience of Quality." *Studies in Higher Education* 42 (8):1455–1473. https://doi.org/10.1080/03075079.20 15.1104659.

Carey, B. 2014. *How We Learn: The Surprising Truth About When, Where and Why It Happens*. New York, NY: Random House.

Carey, K. 2019. "The Creeping Capitalist Takeover of Higher Education: The Corporations Devouring America's colleges." *Huffington Post*. www.huffpost. com/highline/article/capitalist-takeover-college/.

Carlson, S. 2021. "Tenure's Broken Promise." *The Chronicle of Higher Education*, March 11. www-chronicle-com.wv-o-ursus-proxy01.ursus.maine.edu/article/tenures-broken-promise.

CAST. 2011. *Universal Design for Learning Guidelines version 2.0.* Wakefield, MA: CAST. https://udlguidelines.cast.org/more/downloads/.

Center for Innovative Teaching and Learning at Indiana University Bloomington. 2024. "Spaced Practice." Accessed on September 30, 2024.https://citl.indiana.edu/teaching-resources/evidence-based/spaced-practice.html.

Chang, A. 2018. "The Subtle Ways Colleges Discriminate Against Poor Students, Explained With a Cartoon." *Vox*, September 12. www.vox.com/2017/9/11/16270316/college-mobility-culture.

Chang, M. and C.J. Brainerd. August 2022. "Association and Dissociation Between Judgments of Learning and Memory: A Meta-Analysis of the Font Size Effect." *Metacognition Learning* 17: 443–476. https://doi.org/10.1007/s11409-021-09287-3.

Child, F., M. Frank, J. Law, and J. Sarakatsannis. 2023. "What Do Higher Education Students Want From Online Learning?" *McKinsey & Company*, June. www.mckinsey.com/industries/public-sector/our-insights/what-do-higher-education-students-want-from-online-learning.

Childress, H. 2019. *The Adjunct Underclass: How America's Colleges Betrayed Their Teachers, Their Students, and Their Mission.* Chicago: Chicago U Press.

Chilelli, C. 2024. "Improve Your Classroom Management Skills." *Ohio University, College of Arts and Sciences.* www.ohio.edu/cas/about/assessment/teaching-assistant-resources/classroom-management-tips.

Coble, R. 2016. "Learning and Course Management Systems (LMS/CMS)." *Vanderbilt University Center for Teaching.* Accessed September 12, 2024. https://cft.vanderbilt.edu/learning-and-course-management-systems/.

Colby, G. 2023. "Data Snapshot: Tenure and Contingency in US Higher Education." *AAUP* 109 (1). www.aaup.org/article/data-snapshot-tenure-and-contingency-us-higher-education.

Cole, N. 2016. "8 Horrible Habits That Are Ruining Your Productivity (and What You Can Do to Fix Them)." *Inc. Online newsletter*, November 6. www.inc.com/nicolas-cole/8-horrible-habits-that-are-ruining-your-productivity-and-what-you-can-do-to-fix-.html.

Columbia Center for Teaching and Learning. 2020. "Hybrid/HyFlex Teaching & Learning." *Columbia University.* Accessed February 7, 2024. https://ctl.columbia.edu/resources-and-technology/teaching-with-technology/teaching-online/hyflex/.

Cornell University. 2024. "Documenting Teaching With a Teaching Portfolio." *Cornell University Center for Teaching Innovation.* https://teaching.cornell.

edu/teaching-resources/assessment-evaluation/documenting-teaching-teaching-portfolio.

Cox, S. 2017. "Building Relationships by Checking in With Students." *TeacherReady Online Certification Program*, February 17. https://uwf.edu/academic-affairs/departments/school-of-education/teacherready/.

Dagnall, P. 2021. "Understanding Extrinsic and Intrinsic Motivation in Your Students." *University of Dayton Blogs*, September 13. https://udayton.edu/blogs/onlinelearning/2021/09_13_2021_motivation.php.

D'Angostino, S. 2023. "ChatGPT Advice Academics Can Use Now." *Inside Higher Education*, January 11.

Dean, C.B., E.R. Hubbell., H. Pitler., and B.J. Stone. 2012. *Classroom Instruction That Works: Research-Based Strategies for Increasing Student Achievement.* 2nd Edition. Alexandria, VA: ASCD.

De Bruin, E. 2013. "How to Spend Less Time Preparing for Lectures." *Yale Teaching Center*, February. https://yalegtc.blogspot.com/2013/02/normal.html.

De Frondville, T. 2009. "How to Keep Kids Engaged in Class." *Edutopia,* George Lucas Higher Education Foundation. www.edutopia.org/classroom-student-participation-tips.

Dettmar, K. 2022. *How to Chair a Department.* Baltimore: Johns Hopkins University Press.

Devereaux, B.C. 2024. "How to Treat Your Visiting Professors: Ten Steps That Departments Could Take, at Zero or Minimal Cost, to Extend Basic Collegiality to Their Contingent Colleagues." *The Chronicle of Higher Education.* January 24. Accessed August 19, 2024. www.chronicle.com/article/how-to-treat-your-visiting-professors.

Dewey, J. 1929. "My Pedagogic Creed." In *The Curriculum Studies Reader,* edited by D. Flinders and S. Thornton, 2009. New York, NY: Routledge.

Dimock, M. 2019. "Defining Generations: Where Millennials End and Generation Z Begins." *Pew Research Center*, January 17. www.pewresearch.org/fact-tank/2019/01/17/where-millennials-end-and-generation-z-begins/.

Diversity in Higher Education. 2021. "The Truth About Tenure in Higher Education." *National Education Association.* https://diversityinhighereducation.com/articles/The-Truth-About-Tenure-in-Higher-Education.

Doležal, J. 2022. "The Big Quit: Even Tenure-line Professors Are Leaving Academe." *The Chronicle of Higher Education.*, May 27. www.chronicle.com/article/the-big-quit.

Dunlosky, J., K.A. Rawson., E.J. Marsh., M.J. Nathan., and D.T. Willingham. 2013. "Improving Students' Learning With Effective Learning Techniques: Promising Directions from Cognitive and Educational Psychology." *Psychological Science in the Public Interest* 14 (1): 4–58.

Dunn, S. 2013. "Why So Many Academics Quit and Tell." *Chronicle Vitae,* December 12. https://chroniclevitae.com/news/216-why-so-many-academics-quit-and-tell.

Duprey, T.A. 2024. "Should Teachers be Tough Graders/ Here's What They Have to Say." *Education Week,* June 12. www.edweek.org/teaching-learning/should-teachers-be-tough-graders-heres-what-they-have-to-say/2024/06.

Eells, W.C. 1962. "The Origin and Early History of Sabbatical Leave." *AAUP Bulletin* 48 (3): 253–256.

Ellwanger, A. 2022. "Contract-Grading and the War against Academic Excellence". *James G Martin Center for Academic Renewal,* April 20. www.jamesgmartin.center/2022/04/contract-grading-and-the-war-against-academic-excellence/.

Fang, V. 2023. "Dressing Up for Exams Can Improve Academic Performance." *The Daily Texan,* April 16. https://thedailytexan.com/2023/04/16/dressing-up-for-exams-can-improve-academic-performance/.

Felder, R. 2010. "Are Learning Styles Invalid? (Hint: No!)." *On-Course Newsletter,* September 27.

Felder, R.M., and R. Brent. 2024. *Teaching and Learning STEM: A Practical Guide.* Jossey-Bass: CA.

Felton, P., and L. Lambert. 2020. *Relationship-Rich Education: How Human Connections Drive Success in College.* Baltimore: Johns Hopkins University Press.

Feynman, R.P. 1991. *The Pleasure of Finding Things Out.* Cambridge: Helix Books.

Finley, T. 2014. "Dipsticks: Efficient Ways to Check for Understanding." *Edutopia (George Lucas Educational Foundation),* July 30. www.edutopia.org/blog/dipsticks-to-check-for-understanding-todd-finley.

Flaherty, C. 2016. "More Faculty Diversity, not on Tenure Track." *Inside Higher Education,* August 21. www.insidehighered.com/news/2016/08/22/study-finds-gains-faculty-diversity-not-tenure-track.

Flaherty, C. 2020. "Barely Getting By." *Inside Higher Education,* April 19. *www.insidehighered.com/news/2020/04/20/new-report-says-many-adjuncts-make-less-3500-course-and-25000-year.*

Fitzgerald, D. 2017. "Our Hallways Are Too Quiet." *The Chronicle of Higher Education.* www.chronicle.com/article/Our-Hallways-Are-Too-Quiet/239406.

Fowler, R. 2019. "Protecting Students or Enabling Trolls? Why Faculty Evaluations Should Not Be Totally Anonymous." *Dan Hirschman Blog.* June 22. https://scatter.wordpress.com/2019/06/22/protecting-students-or-enabling-trolls-why-faculty-evaluations-should-not-be-totally-anonymous/.

Fulk, A.B. 2019. "Confronting Biases Against Adjunct Faculty." *Inside Higher Education.* February 13. www.insidehighered.com/advice/2019/02/14/

how-bias-toward-adjuncts-plays-out-among-students-other-faculty-and-administrators.

Franke, M. March 2018. "Final Exam Weighting As Part of Course Design." Teaching and Learning Inquiry 6 (1):91–103. https://doi.org/10.20343/teachlearninqu.6.1.9.

Gardner, S.K. June 2016. "Mentoring the Millennial Faculty Member." *The Department Chair* 27 (1): 6–8.

Gladwell, M. 2002. *The Tipping Point: How Little Things Can Make a Big Difference.* New York, NY: Little, Brown and Company.

Gmelch, W. 2015. "The Call for Leadership: Why Chairs Serve, What They Do, and How Long They Should Serve." *AKA Monographs: Leading and Managing the Kinesiology Department* 1 (1): 1–12.

Golden, J.C. 2016. "Why I Want My Kids to Major in English." *The Buffalo News,* June 19.

Golay, K. 1982. *Learning Patterns and Temperament Styles.* Manas Systems.

Gooblar, D. 2019. *The Missing Course: Everything They Never Taught you About College Teaching.* Cambridge: Harvard University Press.

Guthrie, R., C. Wyrick, C.J. Navarrete. October–December 2019. "Adjunct Faculty Can Increase Student Success." *Planning for Higher Education Journal* 48 (1) www.scup.org/resource/adjunct-faculty-can-increase-student-success/.

Gutkin, L. 2023. "Course Evaluations Are Garbage Science." *The Chronicle of Higher Education. The Review Newsletter.* www.chronicle.com/newsletter/the-review/2023-12-04.

Gwynedd Mercy University. 2024. "How to Become a College President." www.gmercyu.edu/academics/learn/become-university-college-president.

Hall, D. 2007. "Fail Fast, Fail Cheap." *Bloomberg Businessweek,* June 24. www.bloomberg.com/news/articles/2007-06-24/fail-fast-fail-cheap.

Hanson, B. 2024. "Uncovering the True Purpose of Assessment." *Learner-Centered Collaborative.* https://learnercentered.org/blog/uncovering-the-true-purpose-of-assessment/#:~:text=However%2C%20the%20word%20assess%20comes,and%20guide%20their%20next%20steps.

Hansen, C. 2011. *Time Management for Department Chairs.* San Francisco: Jossey-Bass.

Harmon, M. and M. Toth. 2006. *Inspiring Active Learning: A Complete Handbook for Today's Teachers.* 2nd ed. Alexandria, VA: Association for Supervision and Learning Development.

Harris, M. 2016. "10 Tips for Teaching Your First Class." Higher Education Professor. August 8. https://higheredprofessor.com/2016/08/15/10-tips-teaching-first-college-class/.

Harvard University. 2024. "Teaching Statements." The Derek Bok Center for Teaching and Learning. https://bokcenter.harvard.edu/teaching-statements.

Held, B.S. 2024 . "Critical Thinking Skills Are Authoritarians' Kryptonite. Let's Use It." *Portland Press Herald*, January 27, A5.

Hegarty, J. 2003. *Personal Communication With Author (R. Sanford)*. Trinity College Dublin, Dublin, December 18.

Hensel, B. 2019. "Be Informed: Are We Testing Kids Too Much?" *Informed Improvement*, February 2022. www.linkedin.com/pulse/informed-we-testing-kids-too-much-bruce-hensel.

Hessler, M., D.M. Pöpping, H. Hollstein, H. Ohlenburg, P.H. Arnemann, C. Massoth, and M. Wenk. 2018. "Availability of Cookies During an Academic Course Session Affects Evaluation of Teaching." *Medical Education* 52(10): 1064–1072.

Hooks, B. 2003. *Teaching Community: A Pedagogy of Hope*. New York, NY: Routledge.

Hoyt, E. 2019. "The 5 Students You Meet in Group Projects." *Fast,* January 21. www.fastweb.com/student-life/articles/the-5-students-you-meet-in-group-projects.

Hutson, M., and T. Peterson. 2016. "Dress for Success." *Scientific American Mind,* January 1, 13.

Insider Higher Education. 2010. "Serves You Right." *Inside Higher Education*. June 17. www.insidehighered.com/advice/2010/06/18/serves-you-right.

Insider Higher Education. 2020. "Barely Getting by." *Inside Higher Education,* April 19 . www.insidehighered.com/news/2020/04/20/new-report-says-many-adjuncts-make-less-3500-course-and-25000-year.

Ismail, S.M., D.R. Rahul, I. Patra, and E. Rezvani. September 13, 2022. "Formative vs. Summative Assessment: Impacts on Academic Motivation, Attitude Toward Learning, Test Anxiety, and Self-Regulation Skill." *Language Testing in Asia* 22 (1): 40. doi: 10.1186/s40468-022-00191-4. PMCID: PMC9468254.

Jarrett, C. 2015. "All You Need to Know About the 'Learning Styles' Myth, in Two Minutes." *Wired,* January 15. www.wired.com/2015/01/need-know-learning-styles-myth-two-minutes/.

Khabarova, E. n.d. "Dual Coding: Exploring Opportunities to Deliver Learning Content in the NTU Online Workspace." *Nottingham Trent University Centre for Academic Development and Quality*. Accessed September 28, 2024. www.ntu.ac.uk/about-us/teaching/academic-development-and-quality/cadq-blogs/dual-coding-exploring-opportunities-to-deliver-learning-content-in-now.

Kelsky, K. 2012. "How to Plan your Research and Writing Trajectory on the Tenure Track." *The Professor Is in*. https://theprofessorisin.com/2014/06/20/how-to-plan-your-research-trajectory/.

Kelsky, Karen. 2017. "How (Not) to Negotiate a Tenure Track Salary." *The Professor is In.* https://theprofessorisin.com/2017/02/24/how-not-to-negotiate-a-tenure-track-salary/.

Keenan, O. 2022. "Rate My Professors' Bias Problem Deserves Failing Grades." *The Daily Targum,* October 20. https://dailytargum.com/article/2022/10/rate-my-professors-bias-problem-deserves-failing-grades.

Keirsey, D. and M. Bates. 1978. *Please Understand Me: Character & Temperament Styles.* Del Mar, CA: Prometheus Nemesis Books.

Knowledge Anywhere. 2024. "5 Strategies for Encouraging Lifelong Learning and Continued Education." https://knowledgeanywhere.com/articles/five-strategies-for-encouraging-lifelong-learning-and-continued-education/.

Kolata, G. 2016. "So Many Research Scientists So Few Professorships." *The New York Times,* July 14, 3.

Kutner, Max. August 2014. How to Game the College Rankings. Boston Magazine. August 24, 2014. https://www.bostonmagazine.com/2014/08/26/how-northeastern-gamed-the-college-rankings/.

Lang, J.M. 2021. "How to Teach a Good First Day of Class." *The Chronicle of Higher Education.* www.chronicle.com/article/how-to-teach-a-good-first-day-of-class/?cid2=gen_login_refresh&cid=gen_sign_in.

Larson, R.C, N. Ghaffarzadegan and Y. Xue. November/December 2014. "Too Many PhD Graduates or too Few Academic Job Openings: The Basic Reproductive number R_0 in Academia." *Systems Research and Behavioral Science* 31 (6): 745–750.

Lieberman, Mark. 2018. "Centers of the pedagogical universe." Inside Higher Education. February 27, 2018. https://www.insidehighered.com/digital-learning/article/2018/02/28/centers-teaching-and-learning-serve-hub-improving-teaching.

Leppink, J. October 2017. "Cognitive Load Theory: Practical Implications and an Important Challenge." *Journal of Taibah University* 12 (5):385–391.

Lench, S.C. 2019. "This Is Not a Test: The Real Root of "Assessment" Will Surprise You." *Future Focused Education,* July 10. https://futurefocusededucation.org/2019/07/10/this-is-not-a-test-the-real-root-of-assessment-will-surprise-you/.

Letrud, K., and S. Hernes. 2018. "Excavating the Origins of the Learning Pyramid Myths." *Teacher Education & Development,* 5: 1518638. https://core.ac.uk/download/pdf/225919021.pdf.

Litterio, L.M. 2018. "Contract Grading in the Technical Writing Classroom: Blending Community-Based Assessment and Self-Assessment." *Assessing Writing* 38: 1–9.

Locke, E.A., and G.P. Latham. 2006. "New Directions in Goal-Setting Theory." *Current Directions in Psychological Science* 15 (5): 265268.

Logue, A.W. 2017. "Why You Should Care About Remedial Math." *Inside Higher Ed*, April 30. Accessed December 5, 2023. www.insidehighered.com/views/2017/05/01/why-virtually-all-faculty-members-should-be-concerned-about-problems-remedial-math.

Love, L. n.d. "Enhancing Learning Using Concrete Examples." *ConnectED Newsletter.* Accessed on September 28, 2024. www.unmc.edu/academicaffairs/_documents/connected/Love_TipSheet_ConcreteExamples.pdf.

Mahnken, K. 2023. "Tough Love: Studies Show Kids Benefit From Teachers With High Grading Standards." *The 74*, March 20. www.the74million.org/article/students-benefit-tough-grading-standards/.

Marwaha, A., M. Zakeri, S.S. Sansgiry, and S. Salim. June 14, 2021. "Combined Effect of Different Teaching Strategies on Student Performance in a Large-Enrollment Undergraduate Health Sciences Course." *Advances in Physiology Education* 45 (3). https://doi.org/10.1152/advan.00030.2021.

Marcus, J. 2021. "Some Universities' Response to Budget Woes: Making Faculty Teach More Courses." *Hechinger Report,* April 30, 2021. Accessed August 19, 2024. www.google.com/url?q=https://hechingerreport.org/some-universities-response-to-budget-woes-making-faculty-teach-more-courses/.

Marcus, J. 2021b. "Most College Students Don't Graduate in Four Years, so College and the Government Count Six Years as "Success"." *Hechinger Report,* October 10. https://hechingerreport.org/how-the-college-lobby-got-the-government-to-measure-graduation-rates-over-six-years-instead-of-four/.

Marshall, K. 2023. "The Semester vs Quarter System in College." *Best Colleges*, March 1. Accessed August 19, 2024. www.bestcolleges.com/blog/semester-vs-quarter-system/.

Martínez, D. and R. Sanford. 2016–2021. *The Contingent Professor,* Podcast. Online at multiple sites.

Mazur, K. August 10, 2021. "A Note on Pessimism in Education and Its Economic Consequences." *The Journal of Economic Inequality* 19: 773–783.

McGlynn, T. 2022. "The Adjunct Hiring Process Is Ridiculous." *Small Pond Science,* November 28. https://smallpondscience.com/2022/11/28/the-adjunct-hiring-process-is-ridiculous/.

McGuire, S.Y., and S. McGuire. 2015. *Teach Students How to Learn.* Sterling, VA: Stylus Publishing.

Mcleod, S. 2023. "Maslow's Hierarchy of Needs." *Simply Psychology,* November 24. December 11, 2023. www.simplypsychology.org/maslow.html.

Medina, M.S., W.T. Smith, S. Kolluru, E.A. Sheaffer, and M. DiVall. June 2019. "A Review of Strategies for Designing, Administering, and Using Student Ratings of Instruction." *American Journal of Pharmaceutical Education* 83(5): 7177. www.ncbi.nlm.nih.gov/pmc/articles/PMC6630867/.

Meyer, A. and D.H. Rose. 2024. *Universal Design for Learning: Theory and Practice*, Updated Edition. Wakefield, MA.: CAST.

Minz, S. 2023. "Can Our Campuses Reinvent Themselves in the Face of New Realities?" *Inside Higher Education,* June 05.

Moralis, S. and S. Dinan. 2022. "The Myth of Multitasking. Why multitasking doesn't work and three ways to increase productivity." February, 2022. www.psychologytoday.com/us/blog/the-therapeutic-perspective/202202/the-myth-multitasking

Mueller, P.A., and D.M. Oppenheimer. 2014. "The Pen Is Mightier Than the Keyboard: Advantages of Longhand Over Laptop Note Taking." *Psychological Science* 25 (6): 1159–1168.

Myers, A. 2023. "Level-Up Your Test-Taking Strategies With These Beginner to Expert Strategies." *EdMed*, March 24. www.edumed.org/resources/test-taking-strategies/.

National Center for Education Statistics. 2024. "'Fast Facts.' National Center for Educational Statistics." *NCES.ed.gov.*

National Science Foundation. 2002. *NSF's Program for Persons With Disabilities: A decade of Innovation and Progress*. Arlington, VA: NSF. (NSF 02-094). Accessed October 16, 2023. www.nsf.gov/pubs/2002/nsf02094/nsf02094.pdf.

Neilson, L.B. 2010. *Teaching at Its Best: A Research-Based Resource for College Instructors*. 3rd ed. San Francisco: Jossey-Bass.

Nietzel, M.T., and C.M. Ambrose. 2024. "Colleges on the Brink." *Inside Higher Ed*, February 5. Accessed August 19, 2024. www.insidehighered.com/opinion/views/2024/02/05/most-colleges-finances-are-biggest-challenge-opinion.

Nilson, L. 2015. *Specifications Grading: Restoring Rigor, Motivating Students, and Saving Faculty Time*. Sterling, VA: Stylus Publishing.

North Carolina State University Teaching Resources Site. 2024. "Rubric Best Practices, Examples, and Templates." Accessed on September 27, 2024. https://teaching-resources.delta.ncsu.edu/rubric_best_practices-examples-templates/.

Northern Illinois University Center for Innovative Teaching and Learning (CITL). 2020. Accessed December 5, 2023. *Instructional Guide for University Faculty and Teaching Assistants*. www.niu.edu/citl/resources/guides/instructional-guide.

Novak, K. 2023. "Unleashing the Power of Metacognition." *Novak Education*, June 15. www.novakeducation.com/blog/how-to-use-assessments-as-a-metacognitive-tool-for-learners.

O'Grady, K. 2023. "Getting a Grasp on Grade Grubbing." *Inside Higher Education*, April 26. www.insidehighered.com/opinion/career-advice/teaching/2023/04/26/getting-grasp-grade-grubbing.

Plass, J.L., R. Moreno, and R. Brünken, eds. 2010. *Cognitive Load Theory*. New York, NY: Cambridge U. Press.

Pope, D. 2001. *"Doing School": How We Are Creating a Generation of Stressed Out, Materialistic, and Miseducated Students*. New Haven: Yale University Press.

Portwood-Stacer, Laura. 2016. "How to Email your Professor (without being annoying AF)." *Medium.com*, April 26. Accessed December 5, 2023. https:// medium.com/@lportwoodstacer/how-to-email-your-professor-without-being-annoying-af-cf64ae0e4087.

Portwood-Stacer, L. 2021. *The Book Proposal Book*. Princeton: Princeton University Press.

Portwood-Stacer, L. 2021. "6 Types of Book Proposals That Don't Get Contracts." *Chronicle of Higher Education*, July 19.

Pusateri, J. 2022. *Transform Your Teaching With Universal Design for Learning: Six Steps to Improve Your Practice*. Wakefield, MA: CAST.

Quigley, A., D. Muijs, and E. Stringer. 2021. "Metacognition and Self-Regulated Learning, Guidance Report." *Education Endowment Foundation*. www. education endowmentfoundation.org.up.

Rawson, K.A., R.C. Thomas, and L.L. Jacoby. 2015. "The Power of Examples: Illustrative Examples Enhance Conceptual Learning of Declarative Concepts." *Educational Psychology Review* 27 (3): 483–504. www.jstor.org/ stable/43548492.

Rogers, E.M. 2003. *Diffusion of Innovations*. 5th ed. New York, NY: Fee Press.

Ross, E. 2021. "Questions That Create Connections: 6 Tips for Fostering Deep Learning in Person and Online." *Remote Summit 2021*. https://sched.com/.

Rubenstein: Rubinstein, J. S., Meyer, D. E., & Evans, J. E. 2001. Executive control of cognitive processes in task switching. *Journal of experimental psychology: human perception and performance*, 27(4), 763.

Russell, I.J., W.D. Hendricson, and R.J. Herbert. November 1984. "Effects of Lecture Information Density on Medical Student Achievement." *Journal of Medical Education* 59: 11 (1): 881–889. doi: 10.1097/00001888-198411000-00007.

Russo, R. 1997. *Straight Man*. NY: Vintage Books.

Savion, L. 2012. "Clinging to Discredited Beliefs: The Larger Cognitive Story." *Journal of the Scholarship of Teaching and Learning* 9 (1): 81–92.

Schumacher, J. 2014. *Dear Committee Members: A Novel*. NY: Anchor.

Schumacher, J. 2018. *The Shakespeare Requirement: A Novel*. NY: Anchor.

Scott, I. 2023. "Yes, We Are in a (ChatGPT) Crisis." *Inside Higher Education*, April 18.

Seemiller, C., and M. Grace. 2016. *Generation Z Goes to College*. Jossey-Bass: CA.

SENCER (Science Education for New Civic Engagements and Responsibilities). 2023. *A Program of the National Center for Science & Civic Engagement (NCSCE)*. https://sencer.net and https://ncsce.net.

Shatz, I. 2024. "Interleaving: How Mixed Practice Can Boost Learning." *Effectiviology*. https://effectiviology.com/interleaving/.

Sheridan, R. 2012. "Five Techniques for Improving Student Attendance." *Faculty Focus*. www.facultyfocus.com/articles/effective-teaching-strategies/five-techniques-for-improving-student-attendance/.

Shmerling, R.M. 2022. "Right Brain/Left Brain, Right?" *Mind and Mood*, March 24.

Strong, B., M. Davis, and V. Hawks. 2004. "Self-Grading in Large General Education Classes: A Case Study." *College Teaching* 52: 52–57.

Sweller, J. August 2019. "Cognitive Load Theory and Educational Technology." *Educational Technology Research and Development* 68: 1–16.

TopUniversities. 2024. "University Budgets: Where Your Fees Go." *TopUniversities*, August 5. Accessed August 19. www.topuniversities.com/student-info/student-finance/university-budgets-where-your-fees-go .

Trubek, A. 2013. "Giving Up Tenure? Who Does That?" *The Chronicle of Higher Education*. www.chronicle.com/article/giving-up-tenure-who-does-that/.

Tuckman, B.W. 1965. "Developmental Sequence in Small Groups." *Psychological Bulletin* 63 (6): 384–399.

Tuckman, B.W., and M.A. Jensen. 1977. "Stages of Small-Group Development Revisited." *Group & Organizational Studies* 2 (4): 419427.

Unamba, E., N.A. Onyekwere, and O.P. Ekwutosim. August 2018. " Influence of Extrinsic and Intrinsic Motivation on Pupils' Academic Performance in Mathematics." *Supremum Journal of Mathematics Education* 2 (2).

University of Arizona Learning Initiative. 2024. "Interleaving: A Strategy in the Learning to Learn Series." Accessed on September 30, 2024. https://academicaffairs.arizona.edu/l2l-strategy-interleaving.

University of Arkansas Student Success. n.d. Left-Brain vs. Right-Brain. Accessed September 26, 2024. https://success.uark.edu/get-help/student-resources/brain.php.

Van der Weel, F.R., and A.L.H. van der Meer. January 25, 2024. "Handwriting but not Typewriting Leads to Widespread Brain Connectivity: A High-Density EEG Study With Implications for the Classroom." *Frontiers in Psychology* 14—2023. https://doi.org/10.3389/fpsyg.2023.1219945.

Wagner, T., and R. Sanford. 2018. *Environmental Science: Active Learning Laboratories and Applied Problem Sets*. 3rd ed. Hoboken: Wiley.

Wallis, T. 2013. "The Hidden Benefits of Being an Adjunct Professor." *Inside Scholar*, May 9. https://insidescholar.org/hidden-benefits-for-adjunct-professors/.

Wankat, P.C. 2002. *The Effective, Efficient Professor: Teaching, Scholarship and Service*. Boston: Allyn & Bacon.

Washington University in St. Louis. 2024. "Designing a Course." *Center for Teaching and Learning*. https://ctl.wustl.edu/resources/designing-a-course/.

Washington University in St. Louis Center for Teaching and Learning. 2024. "Using Retrieval Practice to Increase Student Learning." Accessed September 30, 2024. https://ctl.wustl.edu/resources/using-retrieval-practice-to-increase-student-learning/.

Watson, W.R., and S.L. Watson. 2007. "What Are Learning Management Systems, What Are They Not, and What Should They Become?" *TechTrends* 51 (2): 28–34.

West, T.G. 2009. *In the Mind's Eye: Creative Visual Thinkers, Gifted Dyslexics and the Rise of Visual Technologies*. Amherst, NY: Prometheus Books.

Wetherbe, J.C. 2013. "It's Time for Tenure to Lose Tenure." *Harvard Business Review*, March 13. https://hbr.org/2013/03/its-time-for-tenure-to-lose-te.

WGU. 2020. "Five Educational Learning Theories." *Western Governors University*, www.wgu.edu/blog/five-educational-learning-theories2005.html, May 30. Accessed August 30.

Wharton Executive Education. 2023. "The Right/Left Brain Myth and More Neuroscience Insight." Accessed September 30. https://executiveeducation. wharton.upenn.edu/thought-leadership/wharton-at-work/2023/05/insights-from-neuroscience/.

White, M. 2017. "Companies Want Tech Skills—and the Ability to Write in Complete Sentences." *NBC News*, May 16. www.nbcnews.com/business/business-news/companies-want-tech-skills-ability-write-complete-sentences-n759746.

William & Mary. 2019. "Practice and Homework: Effective Teaching Strategies, Consideration Packet." *College of William and Mary*. https://education. wm.edu/centers/ttac/documents/packets/practicehomeworkpacket.pdf.

Williams, C.P. 2019. "This School Didn't Teach to the Test—and Scored Better." *The Century Foundation* , December 11. https://tcf.org/content/commentary/school-didnt-teach-test-scored-better/?agreed=1.

Woodbury, R. 2008. "From the Traditional Lecture Toward Dialogical Learning: Changing Patterns in the Teaching of History." In *Ideas that Work in College Teaching*, R.L. Badger, ed. Albany: State University of New York Press.

Worthen, M. 2017. "U Can't Talk to Ur Professor Like This." *The New York Times*, May 13. www.nytimes.com/2017/05/13/opinion/sunday/u-cant-talk-to-ur-professor-like-this.html.

Wright, M.C. 2023. *Centers for Teaching and Learning: The New Landscape in Higher Education*. Baltimore: Johns Hopkins University Press.

Wright, M. 2019. "Why You Should not Become an Adjunct—Yet." *University Business Digital Magazine*, November 1. https://universitybusiness.com/why-you-should-not-become-an-adjunct-yet/.

Wright, S. 2014. "Are You Ready to Join the Slow Education Movement?" *Powerful Learning Practice*, August 12. https://plpnetwork.com/2014/08/26/time-fight-slow-education/.

Yakoboski, P. 2019. "Panel: The Adjunct Faculty Experience: Is What We "Know" Correct?," *Journal of Collective Bargaining in the Academy.* Vol. 0, Article 52.

Yin, S., F. Chen and H. Chang. June 22, 2022. "Assessment as Learning: How Does Peer Assessment Function in Students' Learning?" *Front. Psychol.* 13:912568. doi: 10.3389/fpsyg.2022.912568.

Yong, D., L. Rachel, and L. Nancy. October 2015. "Why No Difference? A Controlled Flipped Classroom Study for an Introductory Differential Equations Course." *PRIMUS* 25 (9–10): 907–921. https://doi.org/10.1080/10511970.2015.1031307.

Zabaleta, F. 2007. "The Use and Misuse of Student Evaluations of Teaching." *Teaching in Higher Education* 12 (1): 55–76.

About the Authors

Daniel Martínez has a PhD in chemical engineering and was associate research professor of Environmental Science and Policy at the University of Southern Maine. He has worked at NASA, at an international energy nonprofit, and currently is an independent researcher, technical consultant, and a tabletop game developer.

Robert Sanford has a PhD in environmental science and is emeritus professor of Environmental Science and Policy at the University of Southern Maine. He was a registered professional archaeologist in a consulting partnership and has worked in government as an environmental planner.

Martínez and Sanford have decades of experience as faculty adjuncts and part-timers at seven different institutions in addition to having held full-time tenure track and research track academic positions. Their previous book topics include archaeology, applied environmental science, and energy systems.

Index

www.ingramcontent.com/pod-product-compliance
Lightning Source LLC
Chambersburg PA
CBHW061210220326
41599CB00025B/4591